UNIVERSITY OF NORTH CAROLINA AT CHAPEL HILL
DEPARTMENT OF ROMANCE LANGUAGES

NORTH CAROLINA STUDIES
IN THE ROMANCE LANGUAGES AND LITERATURES

Founder: URBAN TIGNER HOLMES
Editor: MARÍA A. SALGADO

Distributed by:

UNIVERSITY OF NORTH CAROLINA PRESS
CHAPEL HILL
North Carolina 27515-2288
U.S.A.

NORTH CAROLINA STUDIES IN THE
ROMANCE LANGUAGES AND LITERATURES
Number 231

THE NAME GAME

THE NAME GAME
WRITING/FADING WRITER IN
DE DONDE SON LOS CANTANTES

BY

OSCAR MONTERO

CHAPEL HILL

NORTH CAROLINA STUDIES IN THE ROMANCE
LANGUAGES AND LITERATURES
U.N.C. DEPARTMENT OF ROMANCE LANGUAGES

1988

Library of Congress Cataloging in Publication Data

Montero, Oscar, 1947-
    The name game : writing/fading writer in De donde son los cantantes / by Oscar Montero
        p.   cm. − (North Carolina studies in the Romance languages and literatures ; no. 231)
    Bibliography: p.
    Includes index.
    ISBN 0-8078-9236-X
    1. Sarduy, Severo. De donde son los cantantes. 2. Semiotics and literature. I. Title. II. Series.
PQ7390.S28D436 1988
863−dc19   88-14376
                                                                                         CIP

© 1988. Department of Romance Languages. The University of North Carolina at Chapel Hill.

ISBN 0-8078-9236-X

DEPÓSITO LEGAL: V. 1.387 - 1988   I.S.B.N. 84-599-2388-6

ARTES GRÁFICAS SOLER, S. A. - LA OLIVERETA, 28 - 46018 VALENCIA - 1988

CONTENTS

	Page
Preface	9
Preamble: Writing on the Border	11

I THE SIGN AND THE SUBJECT

1. Chain of signs and heteronomous subject: notes for a vade mecum 27
2. Narrative sequence and the fading subject 43

II CHARACTER, AUTHOR, AND SUBJECT

1. Models of characterization: textuality and biographical alibi 73
2. Characterization and the elided subject 89

III WRITING: THE AFFECTIVE MARK

1. The play's the thing 115
2. Parting glances 129

Selected Bibliography

1. By Sarduy 143
2. About Sarduy 144
3. Works consulted 146

For Lilia and T. J.

PREFACE

A version of some of the pages that follow was part of a dissertation presented at the University of North Carolina at Chapel Hill, specifically the first sections of parts I and II, which contain background notes prefatory to the subsequent reading of Sarduy's novel. The terms discussed in those sections have gained common currency, but I retain them as the record of an initial approach to Sarduy. The reader of Sarduy may consider these pages a sort of companion to *De donde son los cantantes*. The second sections of parts I and II, and both sections in part III present a reading of the novel, a further layering, to borrow the useful dermal metaphor. It is a reading based on no particular method, but rather on the faith that the text contains legible, coherent patterns, that commentary is an ongoing interrogation, not a set of answers. I have relied on the collegiate *explication de texte* as much as on anything else, focusing on certain salient patterns, on the allusive process in *De donde son los cantantes,* on its legible tics.

Parts I and II suggest that there is first theory, then practice, perhaps the necessary legacy of academic commentaries. Sarduy's work radically undermines such a progression, and puts the critic in that mythical spot: between a rock and a hard place. On the one hand, he may follow some of the leads in the text and establish a reading pattern, which the novel subsequently unravels, pulling out the proverbial rug, leaving the reader stranded; on the other hand, he may allow the style of the work to infuse his writing, ending up with a poor parodic negative of Sarduy. In Part III, to undermine the dualities of the first two parts, the boundaries between theory and practice become more porous, less onerous. I have tried to base my readings on patterns suggested by the novel, elaborating on them by bringing in other texts, other readings of Sarduy's novel, and other works to which the novel alludes, abandoning the whole thing when it begins to harden, going on to a next step, suggesting other possible readings. The line I have taken follows, as much as possible, a pragmatic strategy endorsed by Auxilio and Socorro at the end of the novel. They pick up the pieces, "con amor, con cuidado."

Writing in English about *De donde son los cantantes* has its disadvantages: for instance, the surfacing of a shared mother tongue has to be repressed; a compensatory advantage would be that the "strangeness" of the critical language creates a certain distance, not the false security of a metadiscourse, but the illusory, yet useful, tracing of provisional boundaries.

I would like to thank my teachers and advisers in Chapel Hill, María A. Salgado, Edouard Morot-Sir, Eugene Falk, and other friends and teachers whose comments were always welcome. I would also like to thank the readers of the manuscript in its first stages, María A. Salgado, editor of this series, Roberto González Echevarría, Sarduy's common reader, and Adriana Méndez Rodenas, whose sharp suggestions transformed the process of rewriting into a fruitful dialogue. I also want to thank Johnny Loflin for his version of the Shirley Ellis classic, whose title I have borrowed. [I am grateful to the George N. Shuster fellowship committee for its support].

PREAMBLE: WRITING ON THE BORDER

In Severo Sarduy's first novel, *Gestos,* the efforts of the perambulating protagonist culminate in an explosion, which transforms an electric plant into a pile of rubble. Bits of glass are transformed into birds, and birds into heavy pieces of metal.[1] In *La ruta de Severo Sarduy,* González Echevarría finds in those pieces an allusion to writing, which he reads in an effort, unique and unprecedented, to outline the totality of the Sarduy corpus.[2] Of course *La ruta* leads to no such totality; it clears ground while showing that there is no all-encompassing critical gesture. What it does give us is a fragmented map, a Sarduy topography, a topos from which to read his works. The journalistic impact of Sarduy's novelty may have waned, but the significance of his peculiar interrogation in the context of Latin American literature is still open to a plurality of responses. The boundaries of his "neobaroque transgression" are still being charted.[3]

When the Cuban Revolution triumphed in 1959, Sarduy was already participating in the cultural life of the capital, collaborating in the magazine *Ciclón,* stormy offshoot of Lezama Lima's *Orígenes.*[4] The eighth of January, the newspaper *Hoy* headlined

---

[1] (Barcelona: Barral, 1963) 83.
[2] (Hanover, N. H.: Ediciones del Norte, 1987) 78-98.
[3] I refer to Adriana Méndez Rodenas, *Severo Sarduy: el neobarroco de la transgresión* (Mexico: Universidad Nacional Autónoma, 1983), which focuses on Sarduy's first two novels.
[4] "Cronología," *Severo Sarduy* (Madrid: Espiral, 1976) 9. The story of Sarduy's Camagüeyan roots, his passage through Havana, from *Orígenes* to the Revolution, and on to Paris, has been lucidly pieced together in *La ruta de Severo Sarduy.*

the arrival of a thousand troops led by Fidel Castro, who would enter the capital "por la Avenida Dolores." Curiously, the figure of a different sort of entering hero and the name "Dolores" cross years later in Sarduy's novel *De donde son los cantantes*.[5] By the tenth of January, the newspaper *Revolución* was appearing regularly; it included a literary page titled "Nueva Generación," destined for the work of young writers, among them Sarduy, whose initial collaboration was "Dos décimas revolucionarias."[6] Sarduy's contributions to *Revolución*'s literary page came to an end when he went to Paris on a scholarship to study art criticism and decided to remain there. In Paris, he immersed himself in the post-existentialist, intellectual hothouse of the early years of the journal *Tel Quel*, with its formalist emphasis on the immanence of the literary text, on the rift between text and referent, on the rewriting of history and the questioning of ideologies which helped to sustain the dominant culture, that in which the tyranny of "the natural" obscured implicit mechanisms of power, which the new literature aimed to subvert.[7]

Paradoxically, as Sarduy's writing developed as a search for a new kind of writing, the search for the retooling of the relationship with the reader, marginal to history and to current political processes, the Cuban Revolution, even as it tried to eradicate illiteracy, called for the formation of a new individual and required of the writer a sense of responsibility toward the revolutionary process as a historical unfolding, one which any new fiction must face and interpret for the benefit of a new reading public, which it must seek to educate and to please, with the emphasis on the first part of the classical dictum. Sarduy's work, by contrast, moved toward a definition of writing as pleasure, a

---

[5] (Mexico: Mortiz, 1967). All subsequent references are to this edition and will be given in the text by page number in parenthesis.

[6] "Dos décimas revolucionarias," *Revolución* [Havana], 13 Jan. 1959: 5.

[7] Sarduy has referred to the Telquelian project in Jean-Michel Fossey, "Entrevista con Severo Sarduy," *Insula*, 303 (27 Feb. 1972). See also González Echevarría, "Interview: Severo Sarduy," *Diacritics* 2.2 (1972): 43; and Efraín Hurtado, "Entrevista con Severo Sarduy," *Actual: Revista de la Universidad de los Andes* 2.5 (1967): 126-127. A summary of the theories discussed by Sarduy, a definition of writing as textual practice, as opposed to a "teleological" history, of writing as a revolutionary project opposed to the spent linearity of literature may be found in Philippe Sollers, "Programme," *L'écriture et l'expérience des limites* (Paris: Seuil, 1968) 8-13.

prelude to Barthes, writing as the defining of a marginal space, a call to a reader, on the threshold of literature's mausoleum of meaning. The rift is paradoxical because the Revolution's call for the commitment of the writer was expressed by many of these same writers in Sartrean terms; the Revolution would make true the healing myth of a reconciliation between the writer and his public. On the other hand, the rising stars on the French scene, where Sarduy would eventually figure, were distancing themselves from the historical guilt of the existentialist writer.[8] The new space where Sarduy's work would be inscribed becomes a narrow ledge, the staking out of a peculiar canton.

Reading Sarduy's first two novels, Adriana Méndez Rodenas focuses on the radical break between the historical processes associated with the Revolution and Sarduy's textual practice. González Echevarría reads *De donde son los cantantes* as a radical retooling of the concept of "lo cubano," a festive unraveling of Cintio Vitier's *Lo cubano en la poesía*, an oblique answer to the insular teleology of *Orígenes*, a prelude to *Maitreya*'s fabled exile's return. *De donde* also lends itself to a reading which would retrace the text's definition of the place of a necessary questioning, where writer and reader, transformed in their silent collaboration, establish a dialogue. At certain points in the process of that definition, the readable marks of a writer-subject surge, a subject sacrificed to the letter, reborn in the reader, on a precarious ledge, the erotic, terrorist margins of the contemporary writing/reading activity. Such a transformation, of the writing subject into a legible surface, of the reader into a marked accomplice, constitutes one of the salient strands of the story in *De donde son los cantantes*, even as the historical background becomes deformed, masked, distanced. Such a transformation implies for Sarduy the incorpora-

---

[8] Sartre projects into an "indefinite future," "le mythe compensateur d'une réconciliation entre l'écrivain et son public," *Qu'est-ce que la littérature?* (Paris: Gallimard, 1948) 157-158. It was such a reconciliation, stated in Sartrean terms, that the writers in the Revolution expected to carry out. In "En su centro," an article on Martí, Sarduy, using the Sartrean terminology which was the order of the day, writes that what is needed is more than "un simple cambio de apariencia," in "Nueva Generación," *Revolución*, 28 Jan. 1959: 13. Such a project as a collective retooling within the Revolution eventually clashed with the individual expectations of writers nursed on Sartre's existential dialectics. In exile, Sarduy opted for a different sort of "reconciliation," subjective and affective, a different pact with the reader.

tion in his writing of references to the workings of the sign and to the role of the individual in the language that surrounds him. The pages that follow point to some of those references, annotating through *De donde son los cantantes* what may have been Sarduy's reading list during his days as a student in Barthes's seminar, a reading list shredded and transformed into the tapestry of *De donde son los cantantes*. Pulling out one of its strands is a reductive move, but one which for the reader of these pages may enhance a return to Sarduy's book, to its "deliciosas plumas de azufre."

The presence in *De donde son los cantantes* and in Sarduy's subsequent novels of the works, for example, of Benveniste, Jakobson, Barthes, Lacan, and Kristeva has often been mentioned by his readers: Barrenechea, Rodríguez Monegal, González Echevarría, Alfred McAdam.[9] Sarduy himself has discussed this in a series of well-known interviews. However, the specificity of those allusions in *De donde son los cantantes,* a founding work when it comes to the question of the Sarduy writing subject, has not received a sustained reading. It is in this novel where the Sarduy subject stakes out the porous boundaries of his parish, boundaries which are retraced but never totally erased in subsequent works. The subjective moves in *De donde son los cantantes* have formal consequences, on characterization, on story, on the value placed on literature, which inform the entire Sarduy corpus. Any reading of Sarduy would do well to emulate the final gesture of the ineffable pair in *De donde son los cantantes,* picking up a few pieces, not in the name of exegesis, but in a gesture of partial recuperation. The reader of Sarduy must dwell in the exploded electric plant, in the ruins of modernity, some of whose fragments are nevertheless readable. Such is the "methodology" that orients these pages, a deliberate dwelling on the borders of a text constructed to defuse any naked aims at penetration, to resist

---

[9] Ana María Barrenechea, "Severo Sarduy o la aventura textual," *Textos hispanoamericanos* (Caracas: Monte Ávila, 1978) 221-234. Emir Rodríguez Monegal, "Sarduy: las metamorfosis del texto," *Narradores de esta América,* 2 vols. (Buenos Aires: Alfa, 1974) 2: 421-445. Roberto González Echevarría, "Són de la Habana: la ruta de Severo Sarduy," *Revista Iberoamericana,* 37 (1971): 726-740. Alfred MacAdam, "Severo Sarduy, Vital Signs," *Modern Latin American Narratives: The Dreams of Reason* (Chicago: Univ. of Chicago Press, 1977) 44-50.

chirurgical extirpations. This critical gesture wants to be neither insertion nor removal, but, discreetly, a sort of collaboration.

Even at his most hermetic, in Sarduy's pact with the reader, whether in *Maitreya*'s inversion of the search for the Lama, or in *Colibrí*'s rewriting of the *novela de la selva*, the chase is always on; it is ineluctably staked out in the realm of the sign, ever driven by the same desire. In a review of *En el cafetal*, Julián del Casal wrote, "La novela no puede ser Historia. Más fácil es que la historia sea pura novela."[10] Casal recognized the outlines of the impasse of the modern writer described by Barthes- the writer "alieanated" from History, condemned to tread the threshold of Literature before being entombed in its mausolem, in its museum, in Casal's case. In 1953, Barthes described the double-edged possibility of a "neutral" writing, an attempt to undo the "opacity" of a writing tradition dedicated to the crafting of elegant, "ornamental" works. Today, Barthes's essay on "writing degree zero" recovers its own opacity, lighting from the inside the very trap it sought to describe.[11] The "neobarroco" of *De donde son los cantantes* returns to ornamentation, to the embellishment of a text which exiles all possible "reflections" in order to measure the raking angles of an ongoing anamorphosis. With Sarduy, there is another turn of the screw: the existential, historical alienation of the writer becomes the alienation of the subject, an alienation which has its own tradition, which may predate the concept of history itself. For Sarduy, embellishing the text does not mean applying an esthetic varnish, the "finish" which makes the crafted work appealing to the buyer; embellishing means fragmenting the text, a constant cutting and retracing which constitute a call to the reader, the other subject who must share the pact of fiction. Casal, who fled his *museo* to the declared subjectivity of *Marfiles viejos*, is surely one of the "clásicos cubanos" that so unhinges la Dolores Rondón, which is not to suggest that the demands on Casal, dying in the stifling colonial city, may be applicable to Sarduy; yet with Casal the dice is already cast, as if

---

[10] Rev. of *En el cafetal, La Habana Elegante*, 7 Sept. 1890. See *Prosas*, 3 vols. (La Habana: Consejo Nacional de Cultura, 1963) 1: 220-222.

[11] *Le Degré zero de l'écriture* (1953; Paris: Seuil, 1972) 65.

the task of each subsequent generation were to have a Sisyphean go at it, in what the poet called "el orden de la ficción."[12]

It has become a commonplace in Sarduy criticism to affirm that his work dramatizes the autonomy of writing and affirms its plurality. Writing is the oblique revelation of the discourse of the unconscious; it creates a person, or a persona, from the fundamental absence of the subject in language. For Sarduy, writing stops being the telling of a tale or the seizing of a memory or a place; rather, it becomes a labor of love, the definition of a space where the writer, ever calling to another, the desired reader, the elusive Mortal of *De donde son los cantantes,* leaves the tracings of that need, of that desire. Writing may not be salvation, but it is a compelling ritual, which remains, however extravagant or bizarre, a profoundly human activity, one in which memory, place, and the telling of a tale, seemingly banished from the legible surface, resurface there, transformed by desire. Sarduy's novel is the tale of such a transformation, an attempt to trade in that desire for the possibility of offering to others a legible surface.

For Sarduy, writing may obliquely undermine the ideology of the ruling class and its system of values. Writing wears down the ideology of a language whose primary goal would be the communication of information. Writing does not seek to communicate meaning, or essence, but seeks to define a different sort of rapport, affective yet distant. If such a strategy is ultimately at the service of the very economy it seeks to subvert, as Jean Franco suggests, fiction still serves to redefine the role of literature, to point to its limitations and its reach in contemporary society.[13] Sarduy's work seeks to sidestep dialectical dualities; it seeks a spot within Benjamin's "mighty recasting of literary forms, a melting

---

[12] Casal, 2: 167.

[13] Jean Franco, "The Crisis of the Liberal Imagination and the Utopia of Writing," *Ideologies and Literature* 1.1 (1976-1977): 5-24. Referring to *Cobra,* Jean Franco discusses the writer's attack on society and society's inevitable recuperation of this attack. However, particularly if one takes into account Sarduy's later works, the concept of "writing" does not so much posit a utopia of language, which ultimately reaffirms the oppressive mechanisms of production that it tries to subvert, as it seeks to produce an alternative space, a viable interstice in the edifice of power.

down in which many of the opposites in which we have been used to think may lose their force."[14]

If writing dramatizes the give and take of different codes in a space that is metaphorically a surface, a seamless platitude, to write is still to judge language, to test it, to punish it and caress it. The writer works "against the grain" of any discourse that masks the sign and turns the cultural into the "natural," that turns a social code into "human" nature, and thus blinds itself to its own prejudices, its own oppression.

In Paris, specifically in Barthes's seminar, Sarduy finds a congenial setting for his development as a writer. It is Barthes who would praise *Cobra* in *Le Plaisir du texte,* calling it "un texte paradisiaque," where each signifier hits its mark.[15] Sarduy's novels question in their unfolding the logic of representational narrative which has given the individual an image of his/her own unity and power reflected in anthropomorphic characters. In Sarduy, traditional characterization, founded on the notion of human psychological "depth" gives way to the making of a subject whose fragmented visage the reader completes.

Yet for all its distancing, at times forceful, at times coy, from the historical role of the writer, Sarduy's works still poses itself the Sartrean question, "What is literature?," its method of production, of distribution, its role in contemporary society. The sublimest word is subject to this economy of consumption. His work, however peculiarly, restates the existentialist question that also preoccupied the novelists of the Cuban Revolution.[16] But for those writers, Soler Puig, Otero, Desnoes, Pablo Armando Fernández, the Revolution provided the context where those questions required immediate, practical answers. Once outside Cuba, Sarduy's marginal position, to the Revolution, to French culture, marks the measure of the privilege, and the limitations, of his works. If he restates the

---

[14] Walter Benjamin, "The Author as Producer," *Reflections* (New York: Harcourt, 1978) 224.

[15] *Le Plaisir du texte* (Paris: Seuil, 1973) 17.

[16] I'm referring to *Qu'est-ce que la littérature?* Méndez Rodenas discusses the novel of the Cuban revolution in this context in "La imagen histórica en la novela de la Revolución cubana: realismo y neobarroco," diss. Cornell Univ., 1979, and in op. cit., "*Gestos:* la historia en espiral," 49-100. See also Seymour Menton, *Prose Fiction of the Cuban Revolution* (Austin: Univ. of Texas Press, 1975), and Julio E. Miranda, *Nueva literatura cubana* (Madrid: Taurus, 1971).

Sartrean question, there is a peculiar echo to his fictional voice, deformed, "synthesized" through filters like the voices in much of pop music. The writer's answer implies a plurality of voices that is the privilege of the kind of textual practice he carries out.

On one level, *De donde son los cantantes* becomes an adventure dramatizing the passage from a Saussurean model of the sign as a double unity, signifier and signified, to an altered model in which the plurality of signifiers turns on itself, where in fact the most glittering of the so-called signifieds is the process of signification itself. The novel takes the limits of the genre, narrative voice, characterization, plot, authority, and cuts through them to signal that process, which is not to say that it becomes the closed, immanent universe sacrificed to the dissections of formal criticism, and its "new," structuralist, or post-structural-ist incarnations. On the contrary, "the process of signification" in *De donde son los cantantes* is also the exploration of the way that fiction, specifically Latin American fiction, incorporates and rewrites culture, the culture of Cuba's street and of the Paris seminar. The referents are significant, yet incidental; more significant is the pattern set by *De donde son los cantantes,* which, after the experiment of *Gestos,* opens up the field for a unique rewriting of culture, Sarduy's twisted version of Darío's urgent cosmopolitan frenzy. Sarduy's second fiction, his portrait of the writing Cuban as subject, remains the touchstone of his subsequent works, *Cobra*'s rewriting of the Orient as holy drag show, *Maitreya*'s anti-Lezamian search for the lama, *Colibrí*'s Icarean flight from the house of fiction, *La simulación*'s autobiographical/representational reverie. The shadow of the writing subject from *De donde son los cantantes* persists in these subsequent works; there is no getting around it.

Manifest in the motifs of *De donde son los cantantes* is the mark of a theory of the sign that has evolved from linguistics, enriched psychoanalysis, and turned philosophy on its head. In the process, the sign as a double entity with a material side that would express an immaterial concept has lost its balance, and what is retained of the model is the signifier, which attains meaning in reference to all other signifiers, not to any one signified. For Sarduy, the emphasis is on the signifier in a model of the sign in which the artificial duplicity "signifier/signified" gives way to a differential role of the sign in which meaning, the traditional place of the signified, and of the ideologies it would serve, is no longer a part of the sign, balanced by the signifier, but an effect of the play of multiple signifiers in an endless, ever replayed chain. Sarduy's novel may be read as a text deliberately placed on that metaphoric balance where the notion of a double sided sign would yield to that of a sign/signifier which reaches meaning by virtue of its association with the entire system, a sign-signifier counting steps on the threshold of meaning.

Returning to the familiar textile motif, Auxilio and Socorro's textual tapestry, it may be said that in Sarduy's novel the references to the sign form but a strand in a complex tapestry in which are woven multiple references, from the early chronicles of discovery and conquest to contemporary painting. By focusing on Sarduy's narrative use of a model of the sign, one runs the risk of reducing the scope of his work, but as long as the risk is recognized, the game is fair, and its aim is not to explain away but to invite another reading, and to point, however modestly or obliquely, to the pleasures of a particular reading.

Saussure's definition of the sign in the *Cours de linguistique générale* suggests a retreat from a theory of language as naming of things and a move toward an affirmation of the complex relationship that exists between the sign and the object named. In Benveniste's *Problèmes de linguistique générale*, the emphasis is on the arbitrary link that exists not between the so-called signifier and the signified, but between the sign and the thing named. Benveniste's assertion that it is only within language's system of differences, of values, that the individual constitutes her/himself as a subject, that the very notion of the individual subject is possible, is the prelude to the Lacanian vision of the writing subject implicit in Sarduy's work.

In Lacan's psychoanalytic writings, explicitly cited in *De donde son los cantantes,* the subject is an "effect" of language, rather than its cause. The subject is not himself the cause, the producer of language, rather it is language that works in him, dividing him in a lifelong process of signification. The Lacanian topic, that without language, without the signifier, there would be no subject in the real world recurs in Sarduy's tale of display and substitution. If the sign is incapable of meaning in isolation, its presence implies that of another sign in the signifying chain, a linguistic fact rendered in the novel as fictional narrative. It is a chain where the place of the subject itself is marked by a provisional sign which holds the place of an always absent subject, which is its trusted lieutenant. The subject is not the privileged manipulator of a language from which he/she can be removed while still maintaining the status of a subject. Rather, the subject constitues him/herself through a series of representations available in a process that has, from a logical point of view at any rate, no beginning and no end. *De donde son los cantantes* is the adventure, the flight of such a subject, a subject who in the process explodes a literary tradition and makes of its fragments a provisional visage. At the same time, *De donde* questions the authority of the writer as producer at the service of an always distant reader, as detached in his activity as the writer was in his. In *De donde son los cantantes*, the reader becomes the subject, "becoming" not as "coming into being," "becomes" as "suits." In Sarduy's novel the supposed absence of the subject demands a reconstitution on the side of the also absent reader, the one who returns the text's errant "cruise."

It has often been suggested that in Sarduy's work the model of the writer as a biographical figure outside the text who orders and controls the movements of his characters, or who breathes "life" into them, gives way to a model where any authorial voice is suspect, where the affirmation of plurality makes of each character a sign for an absent author in a discourse to which neither author nor reader properly have access except through a process of relay and substitution. Such moves are not new with Sarduy; one thinks of Unamuno, Macedonio Fernández, and inevitably Borges.[17] Yet with Sarduy, something does change, something does snap in the machinery, unhinging the crisp dualities that made a "Borges y yo" possible. In *De donde* it is not merely a question of multiple authorial voices, of willful characters questioning their creator, of a sharply defined duplicity between life and the letter. The novel posits the dismantling of authorial voice, narrator, pronominal shifts, characters, as viable narrative devices. Those elements are there, but once shattered, when they are pieced back together, they spell out a different order. The novel

---

[17] See Roberto Echavarren, "Literariedad y transgresión: Unamuno, Macedonio Fernández, Borges," *Enlace* 2 (1985).

may then be read as the passage of an ongoing subjectivity, itself shattered as soon as it gels.

However, thematically, it is through characterization that the text dramatizes the plurality of voices that compose it. In Sarduy's work the characters divide and multiply to suggest the dismantling of the illusory unity of the author and the affirmation of a plurality insured by the text itself: the only vehicle available to any writer for whom the act of writing, its very beginning, is the recognition of a shattering of the notion of a unified self and the entrance into the fragmented continuity of discourse. In the modern tradition, Forster's psychologically round character is the kingpin of the novel as the revelation of an inner reality, the private self as refuge and stronghold in the chaotic avalanche of the outside. In *De donde,* such a character is turned inside out, flattened into surface, forced into molds (remember Cobra's feet), transformed into a Bunraku doll, whose gestures are coded in a tradition, whose limbs are manipulated by visible, blank-faced handlers.

The role of the author in relation to the figures that make up his text ultimately involves in Sarduy's work an alteration of a model of the author, of the idea of the body in relation to the text. On the one hand is the model of the author as anthropomorphic figure, inseparable from the man, who from a privileged position controls the moves of the characters. On the other hand, an alternative authorial model undermines this causal relationship by changing hidden cause into legible link, by transforming author into writing subject, an element in a textual body in which a scriptural activity is read, in which the writing subject, as much the product of reading as of writing, is constituted. The subject inscribes the body as legible fragment; the writing activity transforms him into a textual body, a legible body offered to the reader.

The activity of writing becomes the construction of a provisional body, ever reconstituted in the process of reading. The metaphor of transvestism has been used to describe Sarduy's work because like the crossdresser who masks his/her sex to present a version, parodical or convincing as the case might be, of the other sex, the writer would transform biographical platitudes into a verbal display refracted to project another visage, more appealing perhaps, more readable. The significance of transvestism in

Sarduy does not depend on the fact that costumes and wigs are present in the narrative, but rather on the fact that for Sarduy, writing duplicates the mechanisms of deceit, parody, and play, whether deliberate or naive, that always enter into the performance of the crossdresser. The crossdresser often "performs," on a stage or in a public place; yet even in the privacy of his/her room there must always be a mirror to duplicate the travesty for another.

In Sarduy the act of writing resists subservience to a unified author-manipulator who uses it instrumentally to achieve an end or another; rather, a willingly plural persona manifests itself in writing, an activity in which verisimilitude depends on a pact not on a representation. The pleasure of Sarduy's text depends not on what the text might deliberately or casually represent, but on its insistence on the signs of a fundamental agreement between the producer and the receiver. Or to refer again to the image of the transvestite, the typical "drag show" pleases not because a man perfectly represents a woman, but because performer and audience are both aware of an explicit or implicit contrast between two systems of signs, femininity and masculinity, and in that awareness resides the pleasure of recognizing the failure of the attempt, often parodic, sometimes serious, at representation. I would like to review some of the underpinnings of that pact in Sarduy's novel.

In *Maitreya*, the phallus becomes the emblem of metonymy, of substitution and displacement. The phallus, always decorated, becomes a hand, the organ of writing, the mock penetration which yields a monstrous text, an "engendro."[18] But if the result is monstrous, the activity, the production of the text, remains affective. For Sarduy the activity is valued over its beginning or end. There is in the works of Sarduy a constant concern with the act of writing, valued over the notion of "literature" as an accomplished, finished artifact of humanistic metaphysics. In his texts there are specific references to writing or to parallel activities, tattooing for instance, as suggested in the title of his book of essays *Escrito sobre un cuerpo*. The role of the reader, the one

---

[18] *Maitreya* (Barcelona: Barral, 1978) 181. For a discussion of castration/symbolic order in *Maitreya* and *Cobra*, see René Prieto, "La ambiviolencia en la obra de Severo Sarduy," *Cuadernos americanos*, 258.1 (Jan.-Feb. 1985): 241-253.

completing the exchange that constitutes writing, is erotic, inasmuch as eroticism depends on the mutual acceptance of a code or a pact and not necessarily on a sexual encounter, which may or may not be erotic, however successful its performance.

That is why Sarduy's writing is at the opposite pole from the pornographic text, in which the signified is ever the same: arousal. *De donde's* affective undoing of the signified dramatizes an erotic exchange within a text which is both ticket of admission and spectacle for the reader, Sarduy's ticket that exploded. In the act of writing, and in that of reading, the individual sacrifices the idealistic refuge of the proper name, the "proper" of the name. The editorial gesture of authority, which inscribes the author's signature on the cover of the book, has its subversive counterpart in the dispersal of letters dramatized in the narrative, in the shattering of the names of the characters in the narrative, Dolores, Mortal, Severo. The illusory unity of the proper name yields to the shattering of a subject who has left his trace in the activity of writing and who demands, in kind, the name of the reader, temporarily captured by the allure of a legible surface. I borrow my title from Lotringer's article, "The Game of the Name," and from an old hit parade tune whose lyrics are made up by adding syllables to a name, changing it into a non-signifying rap, which nevertheless returns to the name that initiated it, a turn in Auxilio's "espiral."[19]

One must approach Sarduy's text keeping in mind that a hermeneutics based on the metaphor of "keys" is self-defeating. The text yields the answer to no riddle; metaphorically, it is all surface, infinitely approachable, which is to say, readable; it may be charted, not deciphered. Any study of Sarduy's text merely insures a constant reprise. If the rift between the writer and history, between his/her task and pressing social, political problems tends to foreclose writing, or at least to make it difficult in our time, it is perhaps the task of the reader to write on the margins of texts, to fill the gaps, to caress the proffered word in attendance for the next installment, which may or may not come.

---

[19] Sylvère Lotringer, "The Game of the Name," *Diacritics* 3 (1973): 7.
Elliston-Chase, "The Name Game," KAPP, 22 Nov. 1966. This recording, sung by Shirley Ellis, was released in 1965 on the Congress label.

For all the author's insistence in his early comments on his own work on the self-sufficiency of the literary text, *De donde son los cantantes* may be read as a kind of autobiography, the refracted tale of a writer's journey from native province, to capital, to metropolis, a territory that is less geographical than textual. *De donde son los cantantes* may be Sarduy's *Künstlerroman,* the staking out of a creative territory in which he inscribes his subsequent works. In *De donde son los cantantes,* the act of writing is also a fundamental act of distancing, an act whose energy depends not on the power of retelling the past, or interpreting the present, but on the vigor with which it inscribes the fascination of its unfolding. What follows is a commentary on some aspects of Sarduy's unique handling of the writer's task in his second novel, *De donde son los cantantes,* two decades after its publications still provocative, still challenging.

I
The Sign and the Subject

1. CHAIN OF SIGNS AND HETERONOMOUS SUBJECT: NOTES FOR A VADE MECUM

Readers of Sarduy's *De donde son los cantantes* have never disagreed that language is the protagonist of the novel, that language is literally at stake. For example, Ana María Barrenechea has described the novel as a struggle between the sign and its referent, a language constantly metamorphosing in a process of destruction and rebirth. Barrenechea also emphasizes the closed nature of the work, its actions unfolding "en el orbe cerrado de sus páginas."[1] The metaphor of enclosure appears proper, for in the work, the sign, transformed into the signifier, seems to engulf the referent, to destroy it, which is to say to turn it into another sign. The terminology has been so useful in dealing with the work of Sarduy, particularly his second novel, that it has acquired the ring of the familiar. Still, as a preliminary step in approaching characterization, authority, and the role of the reader in Sarduy's novel, I would like to review some of the assumptions about the sign on which those aspects of the novel are grounded.

The work of Saussure was part of an international climate of intense research in the second half of the nineteenth century on the nature of language. The richness of the arguments displayed in the celebrated *Cours de linguistique générale* has sparked polemics and discussions on every level of linguistic studies, resulting in some cases in the creation of new disciplines or in the fruitful fusion of old ones. A distinction fundamental to Saussure's work is that between the notion of language as the naming

---

[1] "Severo Sarduy o la aventura textual," *Textos hispanoamericanos* (Caracas: Monte Ávila, 1978) 221-234.

of objects and a view of language as a system subject to its own order, "son ordre propre."[2] Another key concept of the *Cours* is found in the first chapter of the first part titled "Nature du signe linguistique." In this chapter, the sign is said to be a double entity, composed of two inseparable components: a concept and an acoustic image. The so-called acoustic image comes to be called simply "sign," but to emphasize its relationship to a concept (tree or treeness) rather than to a thing (the tree), Saussure divides the sign into parts which he names "signified," the concept, and "signifier," the acoustic image, the outward form of the sign (97-100). The familiar division, the teacher's example rather than a hard formula, recorded by Saussure's students, may not have been the parting of the seas, but its fissure of the sign became the open prairie where contemporary debates concering the nature of language have freely roamed.

Another aspect of Saussure's model of the sign is that the relationship between the signifier and the signified is not naturally motivated. The sign is arbitrary. There is no manifest causality between a concept and its corresponding acoustic image, which is not to say that an individual may choose whatever signifier he wishes to designate a concept, since language is shared, collective, social, and does not readily admit willful, idiosyncratic changes. In such a model of language, the implications for the writer, the one who consciously handles language, already begin to become apparent.

In Chapter IV of the *Cours,* "La valeur linguistique," the inseparable nature of the two "sides" of the sign is emphasized through the metaphor of the sign as a sheet of paper in which the concept, signified, is one side, and the sound, signifier, the other. Since this relationship is arbitrary, the value of a sign cannot be imposed from outside of language, but depends on the relationship of all signs one to the other. Saussure emphasizes this dependence, without which the sign would not be a sign but an isolated marker. For Saussure, the concept of value in language, the dependence of a given sign on the entire system, suggests that to consider a term as merely the union of a sound with a given

---

[2] Ferdinand de Saussure, *Cours de linguistique générale,* ed Taulio de Mauro (Paris: Payot, 1972) 34, 43. Subsequent references will be given in the text in parenthesis.

concept is a "grande illusion," the illusion of attempting to privilege one term by isolating it from the entire system, which alone gives it meaning, (157). Language is a "system" all of whose terms are interdependent, "solidaires" in relation to one another, a system in which the value of a term depends on the "simultaneous presence" of all the others, (159). "Arbitrary" and "differential" are thus two correlative qualities of the Saussurean sign. In Saussure's scheme, the means of producing the sign, the voice or writing, do not alter its fundamental structure, in which meaning is correlated to difference from the system, a point developed by Derrida in his meditation on writing as the tracing of difference.

Saussure's schematic division of the sign into the concept or signified and the form or signifier has put him for some in the camp of the "conventionalists" for whom an "extra-linguistic reality" is the source of the concept in the signified.[3] In discussing this view of language as naming in *Problèmes de la linguistique générale*, Benveniste emphasizes in Saussure the impossibility of conceiving of an autonomous signified. He titles one of the chapters in *Problèmes*, "Nature du signe linguistique," the same title used by Saussure. Benveniste points out that there is a contradiction in Saussure when he introduces "the thing" as removed from the dyadic sign. For Benveniste the link between signifier and signified is not arbitrary, but necessary. What is arbitratry is that one sign, and not another, is applied to a particular thing in the real world.[4] That is, the question for anyone who deals with the workings of language lies in the nature of the relationship that exists between "reality" and the sign. Benveniste shows that in spite of the claims that some nominalists have on Saussure, one thing is certain in the *Cours:* value in language is determined intrinsically by comparison and contrast, (I, 54).

Saussure assigns the divided sign, which attains its status, its value, in relation to the system to which it belongs, two "spheres" of operation, described in the chapter titled "Rapports syntagma-

---

[3] For example, by Ullman, *The Principles of Semantics*, 2nd ed. (Glasgow-Oxford: 1959), in Saussure 444.

[4] 2 vols. (Paris: Gallimard, 1966) 1:52. Subsequent references will be made in the text using the Roman numeral for the volume, as it appears in *Problèmes*, and the page number in parenthesis.

tiques et rapports associatifs." In one sphere, the sign may appear in a series, a *"syntagme,"* thus acquiring its value in relation to what comes before or after, or both, (170-171). In the other, each term in the syntagmatic chain evokes other signs outside the chain to which it is related by various associations, thus forming with these absent terms associative or paradigmatic rapports.

The two spheres, syntagmatic/paradigmatic, give each sign a floating value. Thus the individual's speech act, Saussure's "parole," the choices that he/she makes must play along the two axes of the available code, Saussure's "langue." Jakobson refers to Saussure's model of language, adding that if there are two spheres of language, the syntagmatic and the paradigmantic, the terms present in a series and the ones absent, each sign must be interpreted on two levels by other signs. One "interpretant," Peirce's term, may come from the context/syntagme in which the sign is found; the other interpretant is absent from the contextual chain, but belongs to the code being used and is related to the present sign by association.[5] Thus Jakobson adds to the Saussurean model the Peircean concept of an elusive object ever approached by a series of signs. Peirce's is a triadic model in which a "representamen" refers to the object by way of an "interpretant" whose role is to interpret what the representamen and the object have in common. But since no single interpretant can do the job, the appearance of one leads, syntagmatically, to that of others. It is this metonymic aspect of the signifying chain that Lacan emphasizes in his use of the linguistic signifier.[6] In *De donde son los cantantes,* Auxilio and Socorro generate a series of interpretants in search of an elusive object, which never "insists" in the chain and whose absence comes to be associated with the gaping Lacanian *manque.*

In his study of aphasic patients, Jakobson concludes that there are those with "similarity disorders," those who cannot produce

---

[5] "Two Aspects of Language and Two Types of Aphasic Disturbances," *Fundamentals of Language* (The Hague: Mouton, 1956) 55-82. Also, "Deux aspects du langage et deux type d'aphasie," *Essais de linguistique générale,* trans. Nicolas Ruwet (Paris: Minuit, 1963) 43-67.

[6] In a course given at the Ecole des Hautes Etudes in the spring of 1976, François Récanati discussed the links among the Peircean model of the sign, the Cartesian subject, and the Lacanian signifier. In Récanati's introductory course, he discussed the common ground shared by the Cartesian subject, Peirce's Interpreter, and Lacan's Signifier 1, 2. Professor Récanati's course was invaluable in approaching Sarduy's novel.

metaphors, one term for another, because they cannot associate a term from the syntagmatic chain with an absent term. Other individuals can produce metaphors, but fail to connect terms to form a chain or *syntagme*. Those with such a "contiguity disorder" cannot form metonymies. Jakobson associates this figure of speech, one term for the (absent) whole, with predication, that is, metonymy implies a linear displacement along a continuum, context, or *syntagme*. In the normal individual both of these operations, metaphoric and metonymic, are at work, with a certain predilection often given to one over the other. In the aphasic individual, one or the other modes is pathologically emphasized.[7] Jakobson is dealing with pathological imbalances in the production of language, but when language becomes the central issue in writing, and when the writer ceases to express essence to become a handler of words, such imbalances may manifest themselves in his work, may become readable as parts of the text produced.

Sarduy refers to this passage from Jakobson in his "Homenaje a Lezama" in *Escrito sobre un cuerpo* and uses these linguistic concepts in his works. According to Sarduy, in Lezama's *Paradiso*, metaphor, pulling with it not one but multiple terms from the storehouse of language, is also displaced, "progresando por ramificación," seemingly becoming one with its origin, "la metonimia de los lingüistas."[8] Such a moving metaphor, "creando infinitas conexiones," quoting Sarduy quoting Lezama, forms a series which constitutes the space of the novel, Lezama's and Sarduy's own, in which "Lo cubano" is achieved not by synthesis, the historical province of the realistic novel, but by "superposición," Sarduy's "neobarroco."[9]

In *Escrito sobre un cuerpo*, Sarduy also quotes from Jakobson's comments on Freud's *Interpretation of Dreams* and on the importance of determining in a dream whether its signifying elements are based on similarity and substitution, that is on metaphor, or on contiguity and displacement, that is on metonymy. As dramatized by the speech of the aphasic, the subject is

---

[7] "Two Aspects of Language and Two Types of Aphasic Disturbances" 76.

[8] (Buenos Aires: Sudamericana, 1969) 67-68.

[9] Adriana Méndez Rodenas, *Severo Sarduy: El neobarroco de la transgresión* (Mexico: Universidad Autónoma, 1983) 105.

constituted at the crossroads of these two planes, one metaphoric, the other one metonymic; it is a system that operates even in dreams, that is part of the pattern of the unconscious. If an individual's most private, most particular utterances are determined by the surrounding linguistic code, if even what surfaces from the unconscious is part of that collective code, the subject ceases to be the cause of language and becomes in fact its effect.

In Chapter XXI of Benveniste's *Cours*, "De la subjectivité dans le langage," he establishes a significant link between language as a system of signs and the constitution of subjectivity. For Benveniste, it is through language ("dans et par le langage") that the individual is constituted as a subject, because the concept of the self is founded on language, "parce que le langage seul fonde en réalité, dans *sa* réalité qui est celle de l'être, le concept d'"ego'" (I, 259). Like the sign in Saussure, which acquires value through contrast to other signs, awareness of the self is also experienced through contrast (I, 260). A differential theory of the sign implies a differential theory of the subject, and in turn the subjectivity of an author is not determined by an "extralinguistic reality," but rather it is constituted in the work of writing, whose legible traces the reader reconstructs.

Benveniste's emphasis on the linguistic dependence of the subject and Jakobson's reference, at the end of his essay on aphasia, to the importance of the metaphoric/metonymic activity in Freud's writings on dreams suggest that the processes of metaphor and metonymy at work in language must also apply to activities in the unconscious surfacing in dreams, which maintain with the waking world a constant commerce. In reaffirming the subject's dependence on language, Lacan assimilates the linguistic process of metonymy and metaphor, as described by Jakobson, to the process of condensation and displacement at play in the workings of the unconscious.[10] In Lacan the subject is represented by a chain of signs as an absence which is nevertheless signified through those signs. The subject is nowhere, yet he is everywhere figured, masked in a sense by the very signs that he produces. Such a conception of the subject is correlative to the process through which a writer is constituted as subject in a text. It is the

---

[10] Anika Rifflet-Lemaire, *Jacques Lacan* (Bruxelles: Dessart, 1970) 98.

workings of this process of authorial mascarade that figure prominently in the narrative threads of *De donde son los cantantes*.

The subject is absent from the provisional totality of the text, but it is by virtue of such an absence that the text, conceived not as the finished product of literature but as a process completed by a reader, is constituted. For Lacan the signifier has "dominance" over the subject, not the other way around.[11] In "L'instance de la lettre dans l'inconscient," he writes that the subject, the "serf" of language, is even more so determined by a discourse in which he is already inscribed at birth, by his proper name. Such a discourse is said to have a "mouvement universel," which implies that the processes of such an inscription of the subject are prehistoric, that the naming of an individual signals the entrance into an inescapable pact, the pact of language, the entrance into human society, into culture, which in Lacan comes to be synonymous with language. The entrance of the individual into human society belongs to a "tradition" which determines the fundamental structures of culture, even before the "drama of history" is inscribed in those structures. Such structures of culture may change only as a function of the language that constitutes them (I, 251-252).

Thus, in giving priority to the "tradition" which initiates the individual into the realm of language, Lacan questions the possibility that a new order in society, a historical order, could produce a new language, an "espéranto," says Lacan with characteristic irony, whose relation to society would have precluded the possibility of formalism in literature. According to Lacan, such an experiment, the search for a new language, did take place in post-revolutionary Russia, only to be stopped by Stalin, who, according to Lacan, declared that "language is not a superstructure," (I, 252). In his remarks on the dominance of the signifier in the unconscious, Lacan responds to the early theoretical formulations of the group *Tel Quel*, with which Sarduy was connected. Their formalism, indebted to the work of Shklovsky, Tomashevsky and other Russian formalists, called for a new literature, while aligning the work of the writer with the Marxist theories on work and production. Hence the willful "novelty" of

---

[11] "La lettre volée," *Ecrits I* (1966; Paris: Seuil, 1970) 75. Subsequent references to *Ecrits I* and *II* will be given in the text as *I* or *II*, followed by the page number in parenthesis.

Sarduy's first novel *Gestos,* his attempt to create one of the "artifacts" of a new literature.[12] At the time of its publication (1963), the novel seemed to want it and to have it both ways. On the one hand, the novel's experimental quality corresponds to the writer's task as a handler of words, a language tinkerer; on the other, its deliberately ambiguous reference to the Cuban Revolution did not jar the revolutionary sympathies of continental intellectuals with whom Sarduy was affiliated at the time. With *De donde son los cantantes,* with the narrative disintegration of the figure of Christ, the symbolic touchstone of our concept of history, the story seems to turn back on itself as if to emphasize its marginality to historical processes, its inscription as a subjective exploration of an aspect of Lacan's "tradition."

In Lacan's writings, the subject is said to gain access to language as a child through a fundamental split between his conscious and his unconscious self, a split that is described in term of the Oedipal stages posited by Freud. By virtue of his/her incorporation into language, the symbolic order, the subject can only have an illusory unity regarding himself. The subject is ever split, never coinciding with an elusive notion of self, deceived in the use of the first person, the decoy of an illusory individuality. The subject's being is thus structured around a fundamental absence, related to the original separation from the mother's body, an absence he tries to manipulate, to deal with, in the language in which he is invested at birth. The subject figures in the signifying chain as a missing element, yet he is not merely absent. He is figured in language by a "lieutenant," literally a "placeholder," a sign that represents him and which does not properly belong to him, but to what Lacan calls the "Other," the language or the code to which the subject is bound.[13] The subject is driven in pursuit of an object that would satisfy his desire, the result of his condition of *"manque"* or fundamental absence/lack;

---

[12] Citing from *Writing Degree Zero,* Méndez Rodenas considers that the "novelty" of *Gestos* corresponds to the effort of Sarduy to counteract the modern writer's historical alienation in society, accomplished through the transformation of the novel into a legible artifact, putting aside its traditional, representational load, p. 28; hence the novel's "experimental" quality, and its peculiar difference from Sarduy's subsequent corpus, in which "alienation" in language is the lot of the Lacanian subject.

[13] Rifflet-Lamaire 129.

but he can no more find the right object than he can find his own unity as subject. As a subject in language, he is destined to an eternal pursuit, a constant displacement along a linguistic context, Saussure's *syntagme,* which lasts a lifetime.

The subject is thus defined in its relation to others, through a shared language; his discourse, more than a tool of communication, becomes the medium through which he establishes a circuit that defines a place. In the Lacanian signifying chain, the common property of all, "I" have the possibility of signifying something other, *"tout autre chose,"* than what that language may say. In this scheme, what is significant, after all, is not what is said, or what is disguised, but the fact that in language "this subject" signals his place in the search for truth (I, 262). Hence Lacan's emphasis on metonymy, as defined by Jakobson; it signals the inevitable continuity/substitution of language where the subject defines his place, because "thirty sails" hides not only "the word boat," but the fact that the connection between the two is established through the signifier, in whose relationship to another, "dans le *mot à mot* de cette connexion," depends the concept of metonymy (I, 263).

Moreover, in the metonymic connection from signifier to signifier, from word to word, the subject makes manifest to others the absence that constitutes him. Another type of rapport depends on what Lacan calls "the metaphoric structure" of language, which implies substitution of one term for another and is associated with poetry and creativity, "autrement dit d'avènement de la signification en question" (I, 274). Displacement and substitution are the lot of the subject in language, and if the unconscious is structured as a language, the individual loses the spiritual notion of "depth" to become a surface of readable promontories, his discourse, and still lacunas, the realm of the unconscious, a changing topography, constantly recharted by the traffic of the signifier.

In "La lettre, l'être, et l'autre," Lacan defines the role of the Other and its relationship to the subject. The Other is what the subject loves, what is pursued, for no amount of self-identity can alter the fact that it is in the Other that the subject finds his truth: "cet autre à qui je suis plus attaché qu'à moi, puisque au sein le plus assenti de mon identité à moi-même, c'est lui qui m'agite" (I, 284).

In "Position de l'inconscient," the role of the signifier is said to be that of representing a subject by means of another signifier (II, 206). That is, the subject never gains access to language except through the signifier, and he is ever caught in this fundamental "alterity." The unconscious is no less a part of the social code, of the Other, than the subject's loudest proclamations; it is in the others that he runs across that the subject finds the fruit of his own offered message. The subject fades as a subject behind the signifier that he becomes; he becomes nothing, but a nothing sustained by the advent of another signifier, provided by the Other (II, 200). The illusory individuality of the subject is a "mirage," his self-assurance also a trick with mirrors.

The autonomy of the subject is a concept that Lacan undermines when he affirms in "Position de l'inconscient" that the fact that "the Other" is the place of the subject's "cause signifiante" justifies the reason why no subject may be the cause of him/herself (II, 206). For Lacan the subject's primacy and individuality are an illusion of language; it is the language of the unconscious that surfaces in the individual's discourse, and this total dominace of the signifier projects him/her unto the Other, the inevitable place of the individual's definition as a subject.

In a lesson titled "Le Sujet et l'Autre: L'Aliénation," Lacan restates his most widely known thesis, that is to say, that the unconscious is structured like a language. With reference to the role of the Other in the constitution of the subject, he says that the Other is the place where the signifying chain leads the subject.[14] The subject appears under the command of the signifying chain, which is always the place of the Other. In the chain of signs, the place of the subject is represented by an absence, and this absence the subject perceives in the Other as well. "Un manque," "an absence," says Lacan in this same lesson, is found by the subject in the Other, even in what the Other suggests in his own discourse (194). Referring to Aristophanes's myth, which explains that man seeks his sexual half in love, Lacan adds that the process of psychoanalysis teaches the subject to search, not for a sexual countepart, but for the part of himself which has been

---

[14] *Les quatre concepts fondamentaux de la psychanalyse,* livre xi, (1964; Paris: Seuil, 1973) 185. Subsequent references in the text by page number in parenthesis.

lost and which is constituted by the fact of his mortality (187). The displacement of the signifier, identified by Lacan after Jakobson as a metonymic movement, is insured by the absence of the subject ever encountered in the Other. Metonymy/displacement/movement characterize a sphere of language marked by desire: "C'est là que rampe, c'est là que glisse, c'est là que fuit, tel le furet, ce que nous appelons le désir" (194). Lacan's "furet," ferret or polecat, is a fitting totem for fleeing desire; in French a "furet" is also a person who looks everywhere in order to find something, and it is also the name of the old parlor game in which the players, seated in a circle, pass an object ("le furet") from hand to hand, while another player, the odd one out, standing in the middle of the circle tries to guess in whose hands the object is hidden. Sarduy's view of language as a chase driven by desire, as erotic inscription, his emphasis on "esa lejanía del significado," Sarduy quoting Barthes, is founded on Lacan's "discovery," on his marriage of the Saussurean signifier with the Freudian unconscious, the lair of desire.[15] In *De donde son los cantantes* the concept of the Lacanian chase of desire becomes, if not an ordering principle underlying the surface disorder of the narrative, certainly a recurring phantasm.

Lacan's notion of "absence/lack" structures the subject's every move. "Speech," writes one commentator of Lacan, "is as dependent upon the notion of *lack* as is the theory of desire."[16] In terms of Freud's theories, the young child's conception of himself as the figurative phallus at one with the mother gives way to the coming of the law, of language, the word of the Father, who through a ritual castration, forbids incest. Thus the child gains access to language, to the symbolic order, as a divided subject ever in search of an object which can only momentarily fill the gap in the signifying chain. In Lacan's controversial model, the Phallus becomes the emblem of a privileged signifier, which signals for the subject an ineluctable dependence on the signifying process itself, which is to say, dependence on the Other who returns, and validates, any proffered message. Lacan attacks psychotherapy's

---

[15] *Escrito sobre un cuerpo* 47.
[16] Anthony Wilden, "Lacan and the Discourse of the Other," *The Language of the Self: The Function of Language in Psychoanalysis*, by J. Lacan, trans. Anthony Wilden (Baltimore: Johns Hopkins Press, 1968) 164.

notion of the "wholeness" of the personality and affirms "the play of displacement and condensation" which marks the individual's lifelong relation to the signifier (II, 108-114). The Phallus is the mark of the fundamental splitting that constitutes the subject as member of the symbolic order of language. In the chase of desire, each new signifier takes the place of the Phallus, to be replaced by another. Neither love nor lust satisfies desire, which the subject only encounters as a split, a schism in the metonymic realm of the word.[17]

The Lacanian Phallus is a boundary term in the signifying chain along which the subject's desire flees. It gains access to the chain as a signifier that momentarily represents its own absence. The object, Lacan's "object (a)," becomes the signifier of a desire cut off from its symbolic reference to a signified, the wish for unity of the subject, the wish to be the original phallus for the mother. The object is chased, in its disguise as signifier, along the metonymic turf of desire, by an ever insatiable subject, insatiable because desire is a function of the very absence which constitutes him, because the disguises of the object fail to mask a fundamental absence.[18] Any object of desire proves to be ephemeral, destined to be supplanted because it is incapable of filling the absence that is inscribed in the subject since his origin, inscribed from the very fact of his "eclipse" into the order of the signifier, his original passage into the realm of language.[19]

The Lacanian model of the subject underlies the narrative structures of *De donde son los cantantes,* the signifying chain of a subject ever exiled from the text, present through a series of temporary incarnations ever open to a next step. The chase for the Other, who would return the proffered signifier, becomes on the narrative level a chase for a virtual reader, pursued by characters whose transformations dramatize the metonymic substitutions which characterize the movement along the signifying chain. If *Gestos* rewrites history as formal experiment, aimed at

---

[17] Lacan writes, "Par l'effet de parole, le sujet se réalise toujours plus dans l'Autre, mais il ne poursuit déjà plus là qu'une moitié de lui-même. Il ne retrouvera son désir que toujours plus divisé, pulvérisé, dans la cernable métonymie de la parole." "De l'amour à la libido," *Les quatre concepts fondamentaux* 172.

[18] Rifflet-Lemaire 290.

[19] *Ibid.*

the underlying systems of an established order,[20] Sarduy's second novel carries the idea of subversion to a subjective level, radically marginal, set in the very schism of the subject, an attempt to make of the telling of a narrative, of the act of writing/reading a replay of the subject's, writer/reader, original split at the entrance into the realm of language.

In Lacan's scheme, what is said is secondary to the signalling of the subject's position in the search for truth. At the level of the text, what the story tells, the content of its *"énoncé"* is also marked by the elements of its *"énonciation,"* which signal the circumstances of the writing subject in his search. The elements of enunciation, present in the *énoncé*, the formal manifestations of a subjective process, may be described in a particular reading of the text, which looks for the "imprints" of the process of enunciation.[21] For instance, the first person pronoun is such a mark of the process of enunciation; it marks one of the facts of discourse whose occurrence may be charted in the reading of the text. In reading a novel such as *De donde son los cantantes*, which constantly figures the process of its own construction, a reader may, for example, consider the use of pronouns which refer to the narrated event, Jakobson's "shifters," so called because the pronoun is said to have a floating, or shifting, reference point;[22] it is language's "empty sign," opposed to the fixed reference of the proper name, Wahl's paradoxical signifier, to which the subject is born and which marks his inevitable entrance into a kind of official register, the symbolic order of language.

While most of us are happily oblivious to such designs, the writer may be said to be the one who brackets, sets aside, the proper name with which he/she has been invested, to assume the shifting qualities of an *I*, never definable in terms of an object, in terms of a referent, as is the case with the proper name, Benveniste's "signe nominal." For Benveniste, the forms of the pronoun do not refer to "reality," nor to "objective" positions in time or space; they refer to the enunciation which contains them; their

---

[20] Méndez Rodenas 35.
[21] T. Todorov, "Problèmes de l'énonciation," *Langages* 17 (1970): 8. O. Ducrot, and T. Todorov, *Dictionnaire encyclopédique des sciences du langage* (Paris: Seuil, 1972) 405.
[22] *Shifters, Verbal Categories, and the Russian Verb* (Cambridge: Harvard Univ. Press, 1957) 3.

distinctive characteristic is to be self-referential. In Benveniste's scheme, if the first and second person pronouns are the marks of intersubjective communication, the third person takes on the role of referring to an "objective situation." It is the pronoun of the non-person, which does not reflect the instance of discourse (I, 252-256). In *De donde son los cantantes* the characteristic "absence" of the third person pronoun, its supposed reference to an "objective situation" is fully exploited; "he" is absent, but ever desired. In the willful nonrepresentation attempted by the text, "he" becomes the emblem of the desire for the very referent which the text pretends to obscure, to veil time and again. In the representational or realistic narrative, the first person narrative voice either partakes of the objective reality of the author or posits the possible reality of a real person who narrates; at the same time, the use of the third person in this type of narrative alludes to Benveniste's "objective situation," thus charging the narrative with all the weight of a reality which is nevertheless as much an effect of language as the typographical displays of a Dadaist poem. The "confusion" between a first person narrator and the writing subject has been the workhorse of realistic fiction, which works "as if... there were a continuity of the referent and the utterance through the person, as if the declaring were only a docile servant of the referent."[23] In *De donde son los cantantes*, the pronominal disarray of the narrative corresponds to the movement in the novel away from representation toward a narrative figuring of an intersubjective relationship.

As in Philippe Sollers's *Drame*, in Sarduy's novel, there is no first person narrative "where a previously stored-up person is innocently restored."[24] His first persons are already third persons, "turned inside out," "un *Il* au second degré, un *Il* retourné."[25] In Sarduy's novel, narration at the service of representation gives way to narration as the byproduct of an intersubjective process signalled in the text. However, the "subversion" which the text would carry out does not depend merely on the playful use of

---

[23] Roland Barthes, "To Write: An Intransitive Verb," *The Structuralists: from Marx to Lévi-Strauss*, ed. Richard and Fernande De George (Garden City, N.Y.: Doubleday, 1972) 162.

[24] *Ibid.*

[25] Roland Barthes, *Essais Critiques* (Paris: Seuil, 1964) 17-18.

pronouns in their different roles as described by the linguist. The "subversion" of *De donde son los cantantes,* its rather enduring "excentricity," depends on a deliberate, and unique I think, narrative version of the splitting of the subject, of his fundamental "lack," in which that absence, the ritual initiation of the subject as such, is intermittently filled with versions from that subject's national history, not in a parody of a nationalist myth, but in a peculir recuperation of it, enduring precisely because it is so severely subjective.

The subversion practiced in *De donde son los cantantes* does not depend only on the linguistic fact that a first person pronoun works as a shifter, signalling the process of enunciation, a technique that may temporarily gall a reader eager for the "innocent" restoration of a real person, but which, once learned, is readily defused. Defined by Wahl, it is a subversion more deeply rooted in the workings of language, one which signals the ineluctable splitting of the subject, his dependence on the Other, the only place of the subject's truth. In Saussure's model, the signifier does not entirely escape the role of "representing" a signified. According to Wahl, Lacan's famous bar between signifier/signified is not porous, but resistant; and signification is arrived at through the "articulation" of the signifying chain, which determines the subject, who is "heteronomous" in relation to it. The desired object is excluded from the chain, although it is its spur, and the position of the subject is excentric, defined through relay, on the side of the Other "du lieu de l'Autre (et c'est celui aussi de la vérité)."[26]

Sarduy's work would partake of the "deconstruction" discussed by Wahl, deconstruction of the "sciences of man" grounded on the unity of the subject and the exteriority of the object, on the autonomy of the subject with regards to language (140n). Rather, the subject is the "non-marqué" that indirectly appears under the signifier as support of its constant display/displacement. He "lodges" in the interstices of the process of signification. Only a paradoxical signifier is ever fixed on the subject, the proper name, his moniker, his handle on the real (135). The loss of the object constitutes the subject's desire along the metonymic

---

[26] François Wahl, *Qu'est-ce que le structuralisme?* (Paris: Seuil, 1973) 132. Subsequent page references will be made in the text in parenthesis.

axis of language. He is barred from "jouissance," pleasure, orgasm, by virtue of the fact that he is only constituted through language in pursuit of the thing lacked, the phallus, emblem of castration, mark of the subject's initiation in the symbolic order, which cuts through the traditional boundaries between knowledge, the realm of science, and truth, the realm of metaphysics. No approach to truth, no science, is exempt from the fundamental "otherness" of the subject. "La vérité," writes Wahl, "ne peut que fuir métonymiquement devant un désir de savoir qu'elle même provoque, et le savoir ne peut jamais prétendre ni se détacher de la vérité ni l'épuiser" (139). In Lacan's scheme, science is no longer the realm of knowledge, while truth is relegated to the level of metaphysics, religion, or art. The pursuits implied in them are not exclusive of each other, for they all partake of the structure of the signifier, structure of two crossing planes, the metaphoric axis of the subject and the metonymic axis of desire. In *The Savage Mind,* Lévi-Strauss writes, "It is therefore better, instead of contrasting magic and science, to compare them as two parallel modes of acquiring knowledge."[27]

The textual experiment of *Gestos,* with its desire to undermine the established rules of the game, with its emphasis on the "novelty" of a new artistic form, opens the way for the insertion of *De donde son los cantantes* in an intellectual movement in which "subversion" implies the desire for the deconstruction of an established epistomology, an established "model of man." It is a movement that has sought to subvert linear, historical determinism and to rediscover a different "tradition," grounded not on a human "essence," itself the historical product of language, but on the fact that the access to any language, any system of signs, is the mark of the individual's humanity. *De donde son los cantantes* comes to its readers as a packaged volume, as the finished product of literature, but the metaphor of closure does not suit it entirely. The referent is not so much sacrificed to the ritual of the signifier as it is a by product of that ritual, a richly inscribed, alluring pact. To read it is to participate in its demand, to open it up, to rewrite its oblique subversion.

---

[27] C. Lévi-Strauss, *The Savage Mind,* trans. George Weidenfeld (London: Weidenfeld and Nicolson, 1966) 13.

2. NARRATIVE SEQUENCE AND THE FADING SUBJECT

In one of his interviews Severo Sarduy expresses disdain for the story, for the telling of a story, tall tale, or narrative; "the magic," he says, echoing Mallarmé, is the blank of the page.[1] Like one of his characters, Sarduy probably uttered such a statement "en soprano de coloratura"; it should be taken with a second-degree grain of salt, as a quasi-camp allusion to Mallarmé's esthetics of silence. In another interview, Sarduy has also said that the last part of *De donde son los cantantes* is "un *collage* en profundidad, un *collage* hacia adentro."[2] There is a kind of wistful thinking in such disdain for the story and its attendant linearity, in the preference for the "depth" of the blank page. There is after all an identifiable narrative sequence in the four sections of *De donde son los cantantes,* a "story" in the broad sense defined by the manuals, "any narrative of events in a sequential arrangement."[3] On the other hand, the concept of the subversion of linearity in the twentieth century novel has become an everyman's commonplace. Yet in *De donde son los cantantes* the "subversion" of story may be not an "overthrow" but an "overturning," a turning upside down, zigzagging toward the Bakhtinian enthronement of Mortal-Christ.

---

[1] Efraín Hurtado, "Entrevista con Severo Sarduy," *Actual: Revista de la Universidad de los Andes* 2 (1969): 127.

[2] Emir Rodríguez Monegal, "Las estructuras de la narración: Diálogo," *El arte de narrar* (Caracas: Monte Ávila, 1968) 280; originally in *Mundo Nuevo* 8 (August 1966).

[3] C. Hugh Holman, *A Handbook to Literature* (1936; New York: Odyssey Press, 1972) 511.

Such a subversion is not accomplished at the expense of narrative sequence, as it in *Farabeuf* for example.[4] In Sarduy's novel, the story is taken over time and again by Auxilio-Socorro, identified as semiotic entities from the start. In *Junto al Río de Cenizas de Rosas*, they interrupt the narrative voice and argue with a mock-authorial first person. In *La Dolores Rondón*, they have the last word over the two Narrators, and in *La Entrada de Cristo en La Habana*, they carry on by becoming the narrative itself, printing letters on their bodies. Undercutting such linear progression is a subjective presence which tends to break the metonymic displacement of the pair, as if the novel reproduced the two planes of language defined by Jakobson, the metonymic or syntagmatic, the realm of linearity, and the metaphoric or paradigmatic, the "deep" realm of substitution, "deep" because it draws from areas of language not manifest in the metonymic or syntagmatic chain. If the displacement of the narrative, mastered by the semiotic pair, is the chase for an elusive object, the other realm, the metaphoric, may be said to be that of the subject, surfacing obliquely in certain spots where the text in articulated, where its "hinges" show, revealing for an instant a subjectivity in progress.[5] Such progress constitutes its own "story"; the novel may be read as the constant crisscrossing of linear story, identified with Auxilio-Socorro, and another "story" impacted in the first, that of the subject who pervades the text, who walks through it, crab-like and elusive, yet readable. Therefore, the reading of the novel is by definition strabismic, to borrow an optical metaphor: one eye reads the story, while the other receives impressions of a signalling subject, coy and shameless all at once, *enmascarado descarado*. Commentary, writing about the novel, must renounce such a privilege; it imposes its own lineary, its own

---

[4] Salvador Elizondo, *Farabeuf o la crónica de un instante* (Mexico: Mortiz, 1965).

[5] Julia Kristeva, *La révolution du langage poétique* (Paris: Seuil, 1974) 317. According to Kristeva, a "rejection" of the symbolic order, the legible order of language, manifests itself in certain "instances" when the identity guaranteed by the pronouns *"je/tu/il"* is rejected or questioned. Such "instances" are key moments, moments of articulation of the subject, "hinges" in the text which momentarily stop/unhinge the signifying process. The subject thus revealed is not one which is easily located in the normative use of language; it is a "kaleidoscopic" subject, coming to light in the passages from one articulation to the next. Fiction may focus on such textual rites of passage.

phantasmagoric rigor, allowing one eye to overlook the other; it is cyclopic, not encyclopedic. Be that as it may, for the time being, I would like to focus particularly on the story in *De donde son los cantantes*.

Jakobson's didactic model of language attempts to explain a complex process at work in the discourse of every individual, a pattern altered by the aphasic disturbances he discusses. In Sarduy's novel, the evidence of such a pattern may not be rigurously charted out, but manifests itself idiosyncratically; it constitutes an aspect of the writer's "style," traditionally defined as the deliberate arrangement of words which "expresses the individuality of the author."[6] The "arrangement of words" constitutes a linear pattern, a story, whose unfolding is cut here and there by marks of the "individuality of the author," marks from the subject which surface from the lacunas into the legible realm of the signifier.[7] Metaphor/metonymy, subject/chain of signs, cut across each other, in a struggle that propels the tale, a step/stop process in tune with the dancing conceit of *De donde son los cantantes*.

In his introduction to *La invención de Morel*, Borges refers to Stevenson's commentary about the British readers' disdain for anecdote and their opinion that "era muy hábil redactar una novela sin argumento, o de argumento infinitesimal, atrofiado." Regarding story (linear sequence) and plot (the causality which transforms action into character), Borges adds that it seems to be the "common opinion ... even in 1940" that "el placer de las aventuras es inexistente o pueril." Borges's sly dissent from this point of view prefaces his own disdain for the modern "psycho-

---

[6] Holman 514.
[7] Kristeva, *La révolution* 318. The legible realm of the signifer is the symbolic order; fiction upholds such an order, and that of the reader. By contrast, the semiotic order is "anterior to signification," *"pré-thétique"* (35). In the modern text, the phantasmagoric filtering of the semiotic into the symbolic is not "camouflaged" as it was in the classic narrative; rather such a passage is made manifest, becoming the stuff of fiction. Auxilio and Socorro are ever situated at the articulations of the text in which such a passage, from semiotic to symbolic, is signalled. Their omnipresence suggests that such a process never ceases to take place in the text. In Sarduy, there is no symbolic moment which is not porous to the insidious filtering of the semiotic. Wherever Auxilio and Socorro appear the symbolic order is upheld; the story goes on. Their semiotic legacy is also manifest, undermining yet enriching the story.

logical" novel, which pretends to be "realistic" and his preference for the honest artificiality of the adventure novel, which "no se propone como una transcripción de la realidad: es un objeto artificial que no sufre ninguna parte injustificada."[8] Such dualities are part of an argument whose academic limitations Borges unravels in his fictional practice. A reading of Sarduy's subversive narrative moves in *De donde son los cantantes* may begin with Borges's opposition of the "psychological/realistic" to the "anecdotal/artificial" in the narrative.[9]

After the introductory *Curriculum*, the other three tales, ambiguously summarized in the final *Nota*, develop three apparently disconnected stories, related nevertheless by the ever-present Auxilio-Socorro. Their function throughout the novel is one of constant displacement, which insures the unfolding of the story and contests the pretenses of an authorial voice weighed down by an ineluctable association with a "psychological/realistic" tradition. On the one hand, there is the "secret personal mythology" of a writing subject which would surface through a narrative style; on the other, the realm of the word, legible, horizontal.[10] By putting the author in his place and by identifying themselves from the start as a semiotic entity, Auxilio and Socorro guarantee the unfolding of the story and at the same time undermine the mysterious, almost sacred realm which Barthes identifies as the "deep" source of the author's style in his early essay on writing. In semiotic terms, such a source would be the realm of the signified the "soul" of the material signifier in the model traced by Saussure's students. The pair is propelled by a sustained conceit: that they are the real "authors" of the text, or that the text writes itself. By mocking all hints of authority, Auxilio and Socorro point obliquely to the place of a subject whose absence they signal, deflating the myth of psychological depth, of the "inner life" which has been one of the precious legacies of modernity, and affirming instead that the place of the subject is inseparable from their own place, the place of the signifier, the

---

[8] Adolfo Bioy Casares, *La invención de Morel*, prólogo de Jorge Luis Borges (1940; Buenos Aires: Emecé, 1968) 9-10.

[9] See Sylvia Molloy, *Las letras de Borges* (Buenos Aires: Sudamericana, 1979) 22-23.

[10] Roland Barthes, *Le degré zéro de l'écriture* (1953; Paris: Seuil, 1972) 12-13.

platitude/flatness of language, that the signified is illusory, that whatever its load, psychology or transcendence, it never enters the "horizon" of language except as another signifier.

The tales that compose *De donde son los cantantes* begin with desire and end with death. The gods have gone, and death takes their place. "Me enviaron la pelona, la cabecipelada, la calva, la raspada, la sola," says Auxilio. Henceforth baldness becomes associated with death; it haunts Auxilio-Socorro and crowns the doomed Dolores, her hair ruined by dyes and processes administered by the pair; her baldness, her destiny, is covered with wigs, also provided by the pair, who flee before death but also disguise it, the signifiers weaving their tale over the gaping realm of the non-marked.

The Domus Dei is empty and death shines in god's place, "Brilla por su ausencia." Socorro pulls herself together with a little make-up and some Yoruba necklaces, associated with the syncretism of Cuban *santería*. The absence of the transcendent God, replaced by Death in the "Domus Dei," is contrasted to the relief that Socorro finds in the syncretic plurality of *santería*, a contrast which is correlative to the textual proliferation insured by the pair. Justo Ulloa has suggested that the Yoruba intertext alludes to a Nigerian theatrical genre in which the story is summarized in an "Opening Glee."[11] Auxilio and Socorro carry on such a "summary," introducing the characters and insuring that the intrusions of the author are kept in check. The semiotic pair must carry on metonymically, even if it takes repetition: "Papa por papa, papa por papa las recoge [...] gatea a lo largo de las galerías de piernas" (15). Their failure is signalled, pointed at, "Dedos nos apuntan, nos ponen asteriscos," as if to suggest the metaphysical impasse of the binary sign. The pair had gone to the cafeteria to "feed" their metaphysical hunger, and the "papa por papa" sequence begins when Auxilio drops her tray, which she ends up throwing in the trash. Socorro shakes her, adding by way of consolation, "No es nada," which is echoed by her double. They are back in square one, signalled, looked at, "Ojillos burlones nos recorren de pies a cabeza" (16).

---

[11] "Contenido y forma yoruba en 'La Dolores Rondón' de Severo Sarduy," *Homenaje a Lydia Cabrera* (Miami: Universal, 1978) 246.

Their solution ("Tengo una idea") is to initiate a fictional pact, to set up, for lack of anything better to do, the generic limits characteristic of the novel. By handing out the photographs, they begin the process of a characterization necessary to fiction. The pictures are offered "con una reverencia" to a potential reader, "destinatario," suggesting that *De donde son los cantantes* will maintain a kind of sanity, a contradictory order which nevertheless upholds the role of the reader in the economy of fiction. Not only do they hand out pictures and candies, but also adjectives and adverbs, "añadiendo adverbios a los adjetivos, genuflexiones a las reverencias" (17). The photographs are a preview of the characters which are to follow, as well as cultural markers, signposts for what may be a contextual reading of *De donde son los cantantes*. In one Auxilio wears a *guayabera* and yellow make-up, the masked "Cuba" of Méndez Rodenas's reading. In another, she is a languid Casalian princess – "por eso tengo esa taza de té decorada con dragones en la mano y en la otra este largo tallo con una sola flor" (17). In the last, she is Lévi-Strauss among the Caduveo Indians, studying facial paintings and village plans: "Lo que me entrega el aborigen es una máscara cuyas líneas corresponden al plano de la ciudad" (17).[12]

By the end of the introductory section, the binary Auxilio and Socorro yield four characters, simultaneous allusion to and deconstructive *choteo* of the Heideggerian fourfold.[13] Part of Sarduy's textual strategy consists in borrowing a term from philosophy and "marking it down" at once: "une stratégie du travail textuel qui à chaque instant emprunte un vieux mot à la philosophie pour l'en démarquer aussitôt."[14] The failure of Auxilio-

---

[12] "Caduveo," *Tristes tropiques* (Paris: Plon, 1955) 171-224.

[13] Enrico Mario Santí, "Textual Politics: Severo Sarduy," *Latin American Literary Review* 8.16 (1980): 158.

[14] J. Derrida, *Positions* (Paris: Minuit, 1972) 81. Sarduy's work is an attempt to put into practice the "textual strategy" suggested by Derrida when he writes that the practice of the text turns the traditional concept of history upside down, yet signals all at once the possibility of a historic "reappropriation." That is why the work of the text cannot be conceptual, discursive, ruled by essence, meaning, truth, in short, centered on a transcendental ego. The text must "overflow" the limits of such centered discourses (81-82). In the work of the text, dualities such as signifer/signified, non-sense/meaning, speech/writing, space/time, and other "oppositions métaphysiques," which upheld the centered discourse of a unified subject, reveal their "impertinence," become *"non-pertinentes"* (41). The over

Socorro at the "Domus Dei" may also be read as the failure of a triadic model of the sign, completed by the absent term, the transcendental signified, which is supplanted by Death. The face of Death, "la Gran Pelona" the Unnamable One, brings to the fore the "impertinence" of such transcendence. The pact of fiction set fort in Sarduy's novel requires the doubling of the signifying pair, their continued metonymy, the constant replay of the doubling sign.

The second section of the novel, *Junto al Río de Cenizas de Rosas* is the realm of the eye, of looking and not getting; it is set in a park on the outskirts of Havana, a place apparently notorious at one time for nocturnal "cruising," "looking for love in all the wrong places" as the song goes. The handy referent, the banks of the Almendares river where the park is located, enters the text through Cartesian negation: "Ni la luna, la perdiz, ni los helechos que blanquea, ni los cuatro animales, ni el vino del viento, ni el agua del Almendares: nada faltó al encuentro" (25). Cenizas de Rosa appears, possibly wearing the *guayabera* worn by Auxilio in one of the photographs handed out at the Self-Service. Cenizas is also Flor de Loto and many other things at once: pececillo/colibrí/máscara blanca/el vuelo de una paloma, el rastro de un conejo/una flor podrida bajo una palma, una mariposa estampada de pupilas" (26). She is "mimetic," "pure symmetry." Flor becomes the emblem of metonymy itself; for her, disguise is displacement, and her being is predication: "Cenizas de Rosa se le vuelve nube, cervatillo, rumor del río entre las piedras." Flor and the General run in circles, linked intermittently by "la mirada": "Así pasa el tiempo de una recitación." This phrase prefigures the emphasis on narrative time in *La Dolores Rondón* and suggests that the limits of the fictional pact have to be upheld, for the moment at any rate.

As a butterfly with eye-like markings, Flor tricks the General, fascinates him, pulls him along. The General's pursuit of Flor structures the narrative, as it dramatizes the semiotic constitution of the subject, who lurks in the eyes painted on Flor's hands,

---

flowing work of the text is thus in a paradoxical position with regards to the fetters of history.

eye-like markings, Lacan's "ocelles," which on the wings of butterflies fool their victims.[15] It is a subject that wants to establish, within the tottering economy of fiction a subjective pact with the reader. An early reading of the novel refers to its self-referential quality, calling it, "ese mundo imaginario interno a la obra."[16] But the constitution of the subject cannot be bound in a self-referential, narrative "world." The referential anamorphosis practiced in the text, its bending of the real, does not make of the novel an enclosed, smooth, aesthetically self-sufficient object. The text of the novel is porous; it filters out an incessant call to the reader. The General, identified with the signifier through Auxilio, "el binomio Auxilio-General," pursues what he perceives as the ideal complement, Flor, but the object of his desire never presents itself except as signifier, as substitute. Flor's mirror, "specular," image is the channel for the General's driving passion, but she leads him to a false object, to another signifier. Cenizas escapes, "dejando al adversario ese doble inasible, esa imagen deshilachada y móvil" (27). On a narrative level, the search becomes a structuring quest, a pattern which is repeated in the subsequent sections of the novel, Dolores chasing power, Auxilio-Socorro following the tracks of Mortal-Christ.

"El lector," so reverentially treated by Auxilio-Socorro appears as a character to question the disorder of things. The "Yo" puts him in his place with "Bueno, querido, no todo puede ser coherente en la vida" (28). The text does not want the famous "lector macho" pushing his load on the text, grounded on the illusion of his own body. The text demands a different rapport with the reader, who need not be "macho" or "hembra"; on the contrary, its role, like that of the "Yo," is a shifting one, and the subjective rapport outlined by the text is of another sort, a rapport which "passes" through the text, but which it does not fix. The verisimilitude of the narrative depends on the effective inscription of such a passage, not on the dualities incoherence/coherence, life/art mouthed by "Yo" and "El Lector."

---

[15] *Les quatres concepts fondamentaux de la psychanalyse,* livre xi (1964; Paris: Seuil, 1973) 70.

[16] A. M. Barrenechea, "Severo Sarduy o la aventura textual," *Textos hispanoamericanos* (Caracas: Monte Ávila, 1978) 223.

Inside the burlesque theatre, to which this section is dedicated, the role of the Director replays the question of verisimilitude. The Director is stoned and "his" reality is different from "ours": "Para nosotros se quita un arete; él se arranca sanguijuelas de las orejas" (28) – metaphysical speculations which are mocked as soon as they are presented. As chorus girls, the semiotic pair appears as "Auxilio Chong y Socorro Si-Yuen," "poseedoras que son del secreto de las setenta y ocho metamorfosis." Their "ever-present" status is contrasted to the repeated insistence of the narrative voice on the duality between that which is told and the telling: "Bueno, pues como iba diciendo cuando me interrumpieron las Llenas de Gracia . . ." (31). The difference between the time of narrating and that of the events narrated corresponds to the novel's constant switching between present and past tense and alludes to what Barthes called the "tragic disparity" between what a writer "does" and what he "sees." But in *De donde son los cantantes* the insistence of Auxilio-Socorro, their interruptions of the narrative voice, defuse Barthes's reply to Sartre's existential meditation on literature.

In *Writing Degree Zero*, Barthes, not having yet formulated his pleasures of the text, replays the moral impasse of the modern writer described by Sartre, his dreaded solitude, transforming it into a tragic impasse – tragic, because the "living languages" of the world exclude the writer, endowed, cursed by History with a kind of writing tradition that is no more than a "decorative tool."[17] But Sarduy's History is not that of Barthes, and his "decorative tool" has to do the trick, if not the job. From this perspective, one may begin to consider the question of "lo cubano" in Sarduy, not as a set of literary, cultural allusions, though that's part of it, but as a transformation of the European writer's "tragic impasse" into the provisional realm of a different "doing" with language, "neobaroque" as a process of inscription and erasure, as the wearing down of historical ideologies.[18] In *De donde son los cantantes* the dualities between a writer's doing and his seeing, between his language and the world are consigned

---

[17] Barthes, *Dégre* 63-64, 154-156.
[18] Méndez Rodenas 137-148. See also R. González-Echevarría, "Memoria de apariencias y ensayo de *Cobra*," *Relecturas* (Caracas: Monte Ávila, 1976) 149, and *La ruta de Severo Sarduy* 68-74.

to a narrative voice, whose limitations become increasingly apparent as the story progresses.

The theatre where Flor hides is the place of rehearsal/repetition, the transcendental locale par excellence, dreaded by Artaud, for whom "repetition" was synonymous with all the demons he sought to destroy: God, Being, Dialectic.[19] What the General wants is Flor as the sign which does not repeat itself, which is not divided by repetition, Flor as a non-sign: "–Yo lo único que quiero saber es dónde está, quién es, por qué no viene, dónde se esconde, dónde" (51). But for all his "cirrosis ontológica" what he gets is Auxilio and Socorro as the double vehicles of Flor's every move. In the theatre, each scene becomes the masking of Flor before the General: "Así se van desplumando en el proscenio. Detrás Flor, la Fija, sonríe, ausente." Unlike Auxilio-Socorro who are "ever-present," Flor has to be pointed out – "Está allí, en plena posesión de su yin, como la viste en el bosque, ¿te acuerdas?" (51). Flor becomes a symbolic manifestation of that which is outside the text, of the object as presence, of the subject's fantasies transformed into a legible tale. But such fantasies do not enter the text except as transformed through language, through the sign, Auxilio-Socorro. With each attempt to enter the theatre, the metaphysical space where Flor hides, The General is met by Auxilio-Socorro whose code word is "Metamorfosis," and who become a veritable cornucopia of signifiers, behind which Flor "es una ausencia pura, es lo que no es." The one he seeks is one more item in Auxilio-Socorro's disjointed catalog.

Flor becomes the emblem of absence, whose place in the narrative is temporarily held by the signifying pair. The destiny of the pursuer is to trick his desire with deceit and substitution, not to satisfy it. His setting is a marginal, nocturnal world, parcelled into "zones" by Carita de Dragón. María Eng comes to embody the General's desire for Flor, and he eventually enters a space which is said to be behind the chain formed by Auxilio-Socorro, "envueltas en una misma guirnalda." The inner place is the place of inscriptions, of tattoos, where María's tattooed stomach matches sailor Johnny's phallus, "rosado y perfectamente cilíndrico," not the privileged end of the series, but the beginning of one, "El

---

[19] J. Derrida, *L'écriture et la différence* (Paris: Seuil, 1967) 360-364.

glande es un caracol o una cúpula rayada en blanco" (43). The General wants access to Flor, to a Message that he thinks dwells inside that inner sanctum; instead, he finds himself "outside," in the parcelled areas defined by the mysterious Carita de Dragón, "las fronteras del Barrio," a divided text. Along with Flor, the General wants a clear fictional pact: "Quiere el doble, el simétrico, el ludión que pasa del otro lado de la escena para darse a sí mismo la réplica –tú y yo–, que se vira como un guante" (39). He wants, here and now, what is behind Benveniste's pronominal shifters, you and I (I,253). What he finds is the "presence" of discourse. Mobility is the name of the game he has entered: "La ve hundirse entre letras" (40).

The story unfolds as a series of openings into spaces where surfaces are inscribed, María's stomach, a man painting in a bar, a fresco in which Auxilio and Socorro appear. To go inside, the General must pass through a Chinese laundry, smelling of the "proletariat" and filled with contemporary artifacts, Coca-Cola bottles, motorcycles, a portable refrigerator, a radio, as if they guarded the entrance into a place where Flor would be the reward. A waterfall in the fresco parts, leading to yet another room. Separated from the work-a-day world of the proletarian laundry, the place of the transcendental signified is presented as an inner sanctum, full of danger and mystery, paradoxically divided into infinity, and finally impenetrable. It can only manifest itself through the theatre, where the General returns in the hopes of seeing Flor, which becomes his one obsession. Defeated, his only alternative is to seek the death of Flor, which he plots by sending her a bracelet, designed to pierce the wrist of the wearer. He waits for Flor's corpse, for the hallowed Object of his search, a non-Sign to be worshipped, to fill his ontological longings. The story moves toward the expected arrival of what Barthes called a Literature-Object, Mallarmé's caressed Literature, ultimately "objectified" by murder: "on sait que tout l'effort de Mallarmé a porté sur une destruction du langage, dont la Littérature ne serait en quelque sorte que le cadavre."[20] *Junto al Río* is the tale of such an effort, the transformation of Literature into an object, a chapter in Sarduy's version of a "History of Writing." The

---

[20] Barthes, *Dégre* 9. According to Barthes, Mallarmé aimed for a destruction of language, Literature would be the corpse left by that destruction.

General waits in vain, while Auxilio and Socorro ransack *La Divina Providencia,* "tienda total," store-house of language whose contents they haul for the next installment. Because Flor, even as a corpse, is still a signifier—"le cadavre est-il bien un signifiant."[21] In a curious echo of Lacan, Walt Whitman writes, "The blank left by the words wanted, but unsupplied, has sometimes an unnamably putrid cadaverous meaning."[22]

In *Escrito sobre un cuerpo,* Sarduy defines *"Lo cubano como superposición,"* and mentions the possibility of treating such superposition in distinct narratives, each dealing with a different racial component, "uno español, otro africano y otro chino" (69). In the *Nota* at the end of *De donde son los cantantes,* the same three cultures are said to structure the novel, "tres ficciones que aluden a ellas constituyen este libro" (151). The second story in the novel, *La Dolores Rondón,* has been discussed in terms of the black element in the novel, characterized by spoken language, the popular speech of Dolores crisscrossing the bombastic, political rhetoric of her lover Mortal.[23] Sarduy has referred to the "privilegio, en lo cubano, de la audición," but it is "audición" passed through the letter, sustained "por los honores locales de la imprenta."[24] If *Junto al Río* ends with the corpse of a Literature-Object, the rigid by-product of the metonymic antics of the semiotic pair, *La Dolores Rondón,* bursts on a radically altered stage as a reading/rewriting of an aspect of the Afro-Cuban literary tradition. One may read in the rise and fall of Dolores twisted traces of the Cuban pre-revolutionary political theatre, which treated themes of political protest in terms of Afrocuban folklore, a waning tradition by the late nineteen forties.[25]

La Dolores Rondón, an elegy constructed from the verses of the opening *décima,* the Cuban folk poem engraved on Dolores's tombstone, may also be read as a peculiar rewriting of one of Nicolás Guillén's "Elegías," particularly his "Elegía camagüeyana," in which the poet who begins "no puedo hablar" is command-

---

[21] *Ecrits II* 181.
[22] *An American Primer* (Boston: 1904) 20-21.
[23] Méndez Rodenas 118.
[24] "Tu dulce nombre halagará mi oído," *Homenaje a Gertrudis Gómez de Avellaneda* 19-21.
[25] Max Henríquez Ureña, *Panorama histórico de la literatura cubana (1492-1952),* 2 vols. (Puerto Rico: Mirador, 1963) 2: 397-398.

ed by his father to do so, "me obligan el perfil de mi padre, su índice de recuerdo."[26]

La Dolores Rondón is the farcical encounter between the writer's existencial dilemma, mouthed by the two Narrators, and its popular resolution through the faith of Dolores in her own progress, her yoruba saints, and, when all else fails, on the saving grace of her poem, her literary legacy: "De mí te dejo testimonio: mi vida escrita en una piedra, junto a mi tumba" (83). On the one hand is the "tragic disparity" described by Barthes, between the "living languages" of the world and the writer's own dated, impoverished, compromised "decorative" tool, inherited from a History for which he is not responsible;[27] on the other, is a popular tradition, recuperated by Guillén in his subjective rewriting of Afrocuban poetry, not a rewriting of history but personal, idiosyncratic memory rediscovered, and transformed, through writing: "Busco en tu violada niebla matinal/ una calle y la sigo/ por entre el laberinto de mi infancia,/ por entre las iglesias torrenciales,/ por entre los machetes campesinos,/ por entre plazas, sangres, gritos/ de otro tiempo."

For Narrador Uno, the word is lame before a lame reality: "palabras cojas para realidades cojas que obedecen a un plan cojo trazado por un mono cojo" (59). In their non-sensical arguments, a dreary repetition rules; they fall prey to the metonymy of the word without knowing it, the cycle of animals present a compressed version of the story: "La Zoofagia Cicloide," repeated by the Narrador, (77), alludes to the "linear causality" culminating in the downfall of Dolores. Their preoccupation with the word must take second place to the unfolding of the story of Dolores, who comes to embody aspects of a regional literary tradition recuperated in Guillén's elegy to Camagüey, the transformation of the birthplace into an imaginary repository of value. Sarduy's version of such a recuperation, centered on the caricaturesque Dolores, is a paen, not specifically to Guillén, whom he may or many not have had in mind when he wrote *La Dolores,* but to a

---

[26] Nicolás Guillén, "Elegía camagüeyana," *Obra poética, 1920-1958,* 2 vols. (La Habana: Instituto Cubano del Libro. 1972) 1:410-416. Subsequent references to Guillén's poem are from this edition.
[27] Barthes, *Dégre* 63.

Cuban literary tradition which has certainly marked him; it is also a gesture of distancing, less parodical or satirical than farcical.

Guillén's Camagüey is a dream: "Es un sueño./ Oh, mi pueblo." It is the sacred ground, "oh santo/ camposanto," a still, distant place evoked by the poet's voice, punctuated, like the end of *Dolores,* by the "voice" of a guitar. The poem has a subtle narrative thread, the poet's walking tour of the places he knew as a young man, punctuated by three *décimas,* whose recurring theme is memory. In the first, the poet's bandurria is "espejo en que yo me miro," which sighs, "al recordar a mi muerta." In the second *décima,* the poet visits his city, "Aquí estoy," and feels sorrow:

> ¡Puñal de melancolía
> este que me va a matar,
> pues si alcancé a regresar,
> me siento, desde que vine,
> como en la sala de un cine,
> viendo mi vida pasar!

In the third *décima,* he evokes the image of his mother. The melancholy side of memory is given in the *décimas,* whose folk roots are adapted to such themes. On the other hand, the rest of the poem is centered on a roving first person poetic persona whose voice is that of the modern poet, the walker of cities with the roving eye: "Andando voy. Encuentro/ caballos soñolientos y vendedores soñolientos." In the introduction to a catalog of town characters, he says: "Repito nombres ya desabrigados,/ a la intemperie; nombres como huesos/ de antepasados prehistóricos." Among those names is that of the doctor, "que tuvo fuerzas/ para arrancarme de raíz." Pulled from the roots of his origins, the poet looks for "héroes no, fondo de historia," not for the heroes of history, that neither the town nor his own past can give him, but for the recuperation of memory, of a personal history. The juxtaposition of memory in the three *décimas,* associated with a popular tradition, with the poet's own mature, subjective voice, sets Guillén's voice apart from an Afrocuban cultural tradition, certainly from the incidental "folk," local color elements sometimes used to characterize it.

La Dolores Rondón, also built on a *décima* from Camagüey's sacred ground, reverses the movement of the poet in Guillén's

"Elegía"; instead of going home, she wants to leave her origins, to become someone else. She wants to be heroic, to enter history through the triumphal arch of political power; that failing, she transforms death into her destiny, determined to be grand come what may, *"No teme ya el tono grandilocuente, las imágenes ridículas, el folklore, la ampulosidad misma. Dolores entra en la muerte en tono mayor, como un día entró en la vida"* (62-63). Everything about her is false; her wigs and costumes go along with her desire for change, and prove to be her downfall, when in the face of the presidential powers, she tries to pass off as an exotic dancer. For Dolores, the return to her home, "tierra que me viste nacer... ¡y de los versificadores místicos!," is marked by a kind of hysterical aphasia characterized by her disjointed, almost "telegraphic" exclamations, "¡Hielo! ¡Ventiladores! ¡Cuánto fuego!" (80) Her story cannot be retraced; there is no "retroceder en el tiempo," which is what the poet does in Guillén's poem, to transform melancholy into poetic affirmation. In "Elegía Camagüeyana," the poet is "forced" to speak by "el perfil de mi padre, su índice de recuerdo." His reward is a privileged image of his mother: "Mi madre está en la ventana/ de mi casa cuando llego." In *De donde son los cantantes,* the severe outline of the father blurs with the possibility of unhinging his place – "posibilidad de lectura radial y de dislocar al padre."[28] In *La simulación* the redefinition of the role of the father is not solemn; it involves disguise, crossdressing, genderbending: "Se nos ocurre, con mi padre, disfrazarnos." The father is dressed like a comical ghost, a tropical version of the Danish king; the son, teetering on high heels, made up with the best trinkets from the mother's dresser: "yo, con los atuendos más relumbrones de una gaveta maternal heredada."[29] They go off dancing, disguised father and son, if not with the mother's blessing at least with her heels, to the tune of a song whose first chords are struck in *De donde son los cantantes.*

Trapped in the Narrators' story, in its ineluctable linearity, Dolores in undone by rhetoric, theirs and hers, by repetition: "¡Toda repetición es retórica!" (79). Their conclusion of the story parodies the kind of narrative in which Dolores's life has been

---

[28] *Relecturas* 142.
[29] *La simulación* (Caracas: Monte Ávila, 1982) 10.

cast: "Hay que atrapar todos los temas, atarlos y desatarlos, coserlos, emparejarlos, mezclarlos, deslizarlos unos sobre los otros, con melódicos sonidos, tripas llenas de viento" (85). The linearity of the story, imposed by the opening *décima,* is embraced by Dolores, whose narcissistic self-aggrandizement corresponds to her naive belief that her life is compensated by the one poem she has composed, her epitaph. It is the task of Auxilio and Socorro, disguised as her attendants, to convince Dolores that her self-affirmation is misguided, that it is in the continuity of language, the metonymy they come to represent, that she should invest her energies; but her "tragedy" depends precisely on her reliance on her overly stuffed self, on her "roundness." When Socorro pleads, "Ven al banquete," where "Todos comen. Comen y vomitan y vuelven a comer," (83) she is calling for the entrance of Dolores into the metonymy of signification. Dolores refuses; her answer consists of a series of first-person declaratives, "Yo velo/ Yo callo/ Yo ayuno."

The downfall of Dolores, of her individualistic rhetoric, matches the Narrators' garbled dialectic, their errors, "todos tus errores, que son garrafales, hidrópicos, ballenáceos" (67). It is Auxilio and Socorro who have the last word. They counsel Dolores, in vain, and bring her, for her comfort, a mango shake, preview of the "Nada batida con leche" of the end. They put aside the Narrator's hysterical repetitions, *"repetitivo y maniático,"* to have the final word, their Nietzschean "¡Sí!"

Called by Auxilio-Socorro to the banquete where "Todos comen," Dolores turns instead to her epitaph, which is given in full once again; in the next section, which corresponds to the penultimate verse of the poem, she has a dream in which she sees a banquet and a series of animals, "loros," and a covered dish with a bullfrog, "un sapo hinchado," with eyes like a rabbit, and inside the lid, a black snake. The Babalaos interpret the dream and give her advice, ("Detente a tiempo"), but the dream spells out her death, and again her misunderstanding has to do with time, "¿Cuál es ese tiempo?" (85). She dismisses the whole thing as a dream, and continues on the way to her downfall. The presence of the animals in the dream correlates to the "Zoofagia Cicloide" which recurs throughout the story, whenever the Narrators express their negative view of the word ("perro-palabra, agua-sentido") enunciated from the beginning, and dismissed by them in order to present the story of Dolores (59). When Dolores mentions that she is an "apuntadora," a lottery bookie, it is up to Socorro to comment on the significance of the animals in the lottery, an interpretation which contrasts with the Narrators' garbled dualities centered on the opposition of words to meaning.

In the lottery, a quasi-underground numbers game popular in Cuba and still found in Miami and New York, each number is represented by an animal or an activity associated with the animal. Used in combinations, the numbers are made to represent short narratives, so that the bettor can relate the numbers to an experience, and particularly to dreams. Socorro explains that the number one is "horse," nine, "snake," and so on, (61). If someone dreams of a horse riding through a graveyard, he might bet on the number eighteen, a combination of one for "horse" and eight, for "dead man." This form of urban totetism is highly metonymic; bookie and bettor sometimes go to great lengths to arrive at a number, or series of numbers, to represent a particular sequence of events. To Socorro's explanation, Clemencia adds, "[la culebra] que se come al sapo, que se come al toro." Substitution is the name of the game, and the game alludes to a theory of the sign once or twice removed from the Saussurean model signifier/signified, body/soul, a model undermined by the "ever-present" insistence of Auxilio-Socorro.

Saussure explored the possibility of a different model for the signifier in the "supressed" text of the *Anagrammes*.[30] In the traditional Saussurean scheme, the presence of the signified, conceived as pure intelligibility, refers to an absolute logos, to a repository of pure intelligibility, which may be appropriated by any notion of divinity or by a wistfully autonomous subject.[31] It is the place Dolores, as mystic poetess and social climber, would occupy, if left to her own devices. Yet even in the *Cours,* Saussure emphasizes the "grande illusion" of considering the sign as the mere union of sound and concept, isolating it from the system where it gains its value. Anticipating Derrida, he affirms, *"Dans la langue, il n'y a que des différences"* (157, 166). However, the metaphor of the signifier as vehicle, as body of the signified, its

---

[30] Sylvère Lotringer, "The Name of the Game," *Diacritics* 3 (1973): 2.
[31] J. Derrida, *De la grammatologie* (Paris: Minuit, 1967) 25.

soul, persists, in spite of Saussure's insistence on the systematic character of the sign chain. The soul/body model goes hand in hand with his judgment of writing, called a poor copy of speech, not the "vestment" of spoken language, but its travesty/transvestism, "pas un vêtement, mais un travestissement" (51-52).[32] In *Anagrams,* Saussure discusses the logic of numbers in language, establishing a pattern of change in certain verses based on the difference between one letter and another. In his notes on "the versified formula," the chain of signs is "cadenced with abstract marks [. . .] that are purely operational since it is of little importance which vowel or which consonant is included in the counting here where everything is a matter of *differences.*" The versified formula, a signifying chain, "reveals itself to be independent of a meaning which endeavors nevertheless to monopolize it."[33]

In this view of language, the fading of the masterful subject troubled Saussure, who in the end allowed the mastery of the subject over his discourse even if he is not the master of language as a social institution. Faced with the possibility of a subject shattered in writing, the Saussurean subject takes refuge in "a nominal reserve," the "proper" of the name, "dismemberment" suppressed in favor of "the fantasmatic unity of the proper name."[34] The self-affirmation of Dolores, her spunky/funky self-confidence, is grounded on her proper name, which she vainly tries to transform on her way to Havana: "de parte de Dolores Rondón . . . Dolores Rondón . . . qué nombre de concejala . . . Dolores de Pérez . . . Lola Pérez Rondón . . . No hay nada que hacer. Somos el nombre con que nacemos" (71), as opposed to the constant nominal transformations of Auxilio-Socorro: "las Llenas de Gracia," "las Culito," "las Divinidades Calvas," "las Baby Face." Barrenechea has counted sixty-five names for the pair.[35] Dolores would have done well to trust the logic of numbers, in her role as "apuntadora." Yet in a sense, her pathos,

---

[32] Lotringer discusses Jean Starobinski's *Les Mots sous les mots: Les Anagrammes de Ferdinand de Saussure,* and contrasts the "two" Saussures as follows: "the 'first' Saussure lays the scientific grounds for a discipline which constitutes the most indisputable fruition of our culture, the "second" inaugurates a practice of the text" (2).
[33] Lotringer 4.
[34] *Ibid.* 10.
[35] Barrenechea 224.

if not her tragedy, redeems her – her ignorance is her innocence. She heads for death, *"(tan despreocupada como si estuviera en una canasta-party),"* savoring the Nothing Milkshake offered by "La costurera," affirming in her way, "¡Qué suerte, después de todo, haber conservado la batidora!" (80).

In *La Entrada de Cristo en La Habana,* Auxilio and Socorro take center stage; the story is their failed apotheosis, their apocalyptic journey from the Spain of the Crusades to a futuristic, yet familiar, landscape, whose signs spell out a kind of no man's urban turf, the prophet's ravaged city to come. Initially, the story of the pair is built through references, veilded or explicit, to Spanish literature: San Juan, Cervantes, Calderón, Quevedo, Columbus, have been mentioned.[36] The list could include other names, and with few exceptions, it would be difficult to pinpoint a specific source. The style of the Spanish part of *La Entrada* may be said to have a single referent: Hispanicity; in the same way that place-names in Proust reproduce what Barthes has called "la 'francité.' "[37] Contrasting with the boundless orality of *La Dolores,* the setting of *La Entrada* is markedly scriptural. The story begins as a replay of Spanish writing, from the earliest known Hispanoarabic compositions to the Golden Age and chronicles of the Conquest, to modern classics, such as Martí. A discreet narrative voice intrudes at one point to refer to news about the pair, less creditable, because it has been "transmitidas por una tradición oral dudosa" (109). Auxilio-Socorro might be "Las dueñas amazonas [que] non viven con maridos [...] han en las fronteras lugares etablidos" from the *mester de clerecía.* They search for Mortal, Don Juan Manuel's "animal mortal razonal."[38]

In *Junto al Río,* Auxilio and Socorro mask the absence of Flor, the elusive, illusory object, never reached, ever awaited as a corpse/signifier, the spur of the process of signification. In *La Entrada de Cristo,* Mortal is the absent term who is the object of the pair's search, whom it is their destiny to revive. They look for Mortal, yet contain him, suspended for an instant in a distant,

---

[36] For example, by Barrenechea 224.
[37] "Proust et les noms," *Degré* 131.
[38] Ángel del Río, *Antología general de la literatura española,* 2 vols. (New York: Holt, Rinehart, Winston, 1960) 1: 35, 65.

pre-scriptural time; they are "zejeleras," poised at the mythical moment when an Arab literary tradition filters into a nascent Spanish idiom. Ever symmetrical, Auxilio-Socorro are an ancient text, "las Princesas son dos saltimbanquis, y el suelo las letras de un evangeliario" (96). They are a text and readers of texts: "Descifran los capiteles vecinos y de esa lectura reciben augurios de La Llegada y paciencia" (95). The arrival of the tapestry signals the transformation of Mortal from desired plenitude into the present sign of his absence: "indicio de su estancia que dejó Mortal al marcharse" (97). Barrenechea has discussed the correspondence between the figures in the tapestry and the characters in the novel, identifying Hipo, from the tapestry, with Bruno, who goes along with the pair in the procession, and the Prince with Mortal-Christ.[39] Méndez Rodenas adds that the tapestry, once split, suggests two models of the sign, the sign as repository of a signified, the reverse side of the cloth, and the sign as "mero significante, texto tupido," the sign of writing whose history the novel itself rewrites.[40] For Socorro, the tapestry is the classic sign, which contains a "message," "Mensaje hilado." For Auxilio, the tapestry is pure signifier, which must be traded at once for something else, to unleash the economy of the sign to which she is so adept: "Vendido sería nuestra fortuna" (97).

The pair carries on a debate over the value of the cloth which is correlative to the discussion about the value of the word carried on by the Narrators in *La Dolores Rondón*. The two argue over "el sentido justo de la palabra" (58). But the Narrators' arguments center on a moral, existential dialectic, while Auxilio and Socorro emphasize the consequences of the splitting of the sign, of the transformation of the tapestry from "indicio" of Mortal into a sign whose fundamental split inaugurates the practice of the text. Left by "el capataz," who also leaves his tracks ("la huella de sus pies callosos") in the dust around Auxilio-Socorro's bed, the undivided tapestry pretends to be a "substitute" for Mortal; it is an objet d'art, a "fetish" which masks its origins. Once split, it becomes a sign whose displacement insures the unfolding of the story. For Socorro, the tapestry's message is metaphysical, a fixed,

---

[39] Barrenechea 231.
[40] Méndez Rodenas 128.

"deep" metaphor of Mortal, which must not be exchanged: "lengua de Mortal hay en ellos. Mensaje hilado; no será canje de colgajos" (97). Auxilio would impose the metonymy of displacement on the tapestry-sign; her laughter may sound like the "colgajos" detested by Socorro; but it is not. Her laughter is "huesecillos en un cubilete, arena que arrastra el río" (97), substitution/displacement. Socorro's metaphysical stance and Auxilio's materialism do not exclude each other; they signal a reciprocal movement which structures the text. Auxilio, "golosa, jamás harta," a glutton of the signifier, wants immediate value from the tapestry/sign, not the deferred value of a coveted signifying chain. On the other hand, Socorro, "la transcendente," believes in Mortal, whose absent body is the spur of a writing practice inscribed in the text. Auxilio insures the metonymy of the signifier; chasing after an illusory object affirms the quality of displacement on which depends the linearity of the narrative, which guarantees the economy of fiction. Socorro believes in the redeeming absence of Mortal, a transcendence outside of the text, "el cuerpo de un hombre, la salvación del alma" (152), the place of a subject elided in the proces of signification, yet ever aiming to surface, on the side of the reader.

The pair is separated in their search for Mortal, each taking a route associated with two broad realms of the Hispanic tradition: one sensual, festive, erotic, identified with Auxilio in her role as a "zejelera"; the other, ascetic, mystic, metaphysical, identified with Socorro as a mendicant pilgrim, "Mendigó. Vivió de pan y agua. Padeció el cilicio. Se aplicó las disciplinas" (100). The two ways, structured by an absence, are the same; they meet, blending with each other, "creyó verse a los lejos, avanzando hacia sí misma [...] Entonces tropezó con Auxilio" (102). Mortal's absence unites them; their desire for him is one. As the reunited, but ever divided sign, their task is to find traces of Mortal, and eventually to make of their textual bodies the repository of a desired plenitude, the plenitude of a pure intelligibility, of a signified/sacred object. However, the desired arrival is deferred, and again the role of the pair is to insure the continuity of the narrative: "Que no se pare el rollo. El rollo ahuecado que es la música" (107). The pair sails with Columbus, singing a *décima* in dialogue form, rewriting the Admiral's *Diary* as they approach the islands. As separate entities, Auxilio and Socorro want a substitute for Mortal, a fetish; in their search, one is metaphysical; the other one, materialistic. As the two meet, both ways come back toward each other, again becoming reciprocal and inseparable, necessary to the workings of the text.[41]

The beginning of the pair's Cuban phase may be read as an extended reference to Carpentier's *La música en Cuba*.[42] The two are surely identified with "las hermanas Micaela y Teodora Ginés," the latter being the composer of the famous *son* that bears her name, according to Carpentier, a native, *criollo,* blend of Spanish and African elements. From Carpentier's treatise also comes the devil-may-care attitude of the pair, that has so often been identified as a typically Cuban characteristic, a polemical topos at the root of the question of Cuban national identity. Carpentier writes of "una suerte de blandura con todo lo tocante a la religión, que habría de observarse, más tarde, en el desarrollo histórico y cultural de la nacionalidad cubana."[43] It is of course not only a question of history and culture, but of language. In one debate among linguists, the sultry Cuban climate has been blamed for our loose tongue, for the disappearing *S* and the vanishing intervocalic *D*.[44] *Cubanear* means to "hang loose," to

---

[41] The tearing of the tapestry indicates a separation between Auxilio and Socorro which must be reconciled if the narrative is to continue. The pair momentarily wants the presence of Mortal in the tapestry as art "fetish": "Pour garder le procès signifiant, pour ne pas sombrer dans un 'indicible' sans bords, et donc pour poser le sujet d'une pratique, le sujet du langage poétique s'agrippe au secours que lui offre le fétichisme" (Kristeva, *La révolution* 64). But the practice of the text surpasses such fetishism. After Socorro's worship of the tapestry (*De donde,* 100), which is divided to signal the upholding of the process of signification, the pair returns to the unfolding narrative. The text "est tout autre chose qu'un fétiche parce qu'il *signifie;* c'est-à-dire qu'il n'est pas un *substitut* mais un *signe* (signifiant/signifié), et sa sémantique se déploie dans une phrase." Therefore oppositions between "sense" and "nonsense" do not hold with respect to the text. To such oppositions, whether "matérialistes" or "métaphysiques," the text offers its own "dialectic," "deux fonctionnements hétérogènes qui sont, réciproquement et inséparablement, des conditions l'un pour l'autre" (64-65).

[42] See Justo C. Ulloa, and Leonor A. de Ulloa, "Leyendo las huellas de Auxilio y Socorro," *Hispamérica* 4.10 (1975): 18-19.

[43] *La música en Cuba* (La Habana: Letras Cubanas, 1979) 36-44. Subsequent references in the text.

[44] See Juan Marinello, "Un guacalito de cubanismos," *Antología de lingüística cubana,* 2 vols. (La Habana: Editorial Ciencias Sociales, 1977) 2:19, and in the same volume, José Elías Entralgo, "Apuntes caracterológicos sobre el léxico cubano" 66. Both relate "cubanear" to the question of a "conducta nacional." Also in *Antología* 2: 178-179, Adolfo Tortoló refers to Pedro Henríquez Ureña's

"chill out." Socorro and Auxilio's *cubaneo* ties them to an oral tradition, but it is an aspect of an oral tradition long ago confined to the debates of academicians, stored in archives, resurrected in a work such as Ortiz's *Catauro,* surely ransacked by Sarduy for the essential lexicon of Auxilio-Socorro, themselves the victims of "el soponcio caribeño."[45]

The absence of Mortal corresponds to the textual presence of the pair, their insistence on the rituals of the day-to-day. If the One turns a deaf ear to them, the only solution is to pay homage to plural dancing gods. The doubles double again, and Rita Pla and Bruno, a couple from some *criollista* novel appear to fill out the precarious limits of the narrative. In *La música en Cuba,* Carpentier writes that as it happened in medieval theatre, the beginnings of Cuban theatre may be traced to the festivities associated with the Corpus Christi, celebrated with farces and processions, a tradition which lasted into the nineteenth century. The procession included angels, devils, lions, tigers, gypsies, and towering over these, the *tarasca,* a huge, monstrous serpent (44-45), "La serpiente que aparece a los elegidos" which opens *Junto al Río.* For Auxilio and Socorro, the church becomes the space of a constant carnival, which culminates in the procession of Mortal through the island, the mock enthronement which defuses the metaphysical load associated with the absent figure. The body of Christ appears in bits and pieces to become the pretext for the procession, a display orchestrated by the semiotic pair and their double helpers, masking a final disintegration, final for the linearity of this text, not necessarily final in a metaphysical sense.

In *Escrito,* Sarduy quotes from Vitier's reading of *Espejo de paciencia* in *Lo cubano en la poesía.* Vitier sees in Balboa's "desenfadado aparejamiento de palabras" a founding characteristic of *lo cubano.* The chaining together of Satyrs, Fauns, Centaurs, Naiads and other fabulous creatures with "guanábanas, caimitos, mameyes, aguacates, siguapas, pitajayas, virijí, jaguará, viajacas,

---

controversial discussion of the influence of climate on pronunciation in *Revista de Filología Española* (1921): 357.

[45] *Nuevo catauro de cubanismos* (La Habana: Editorial de Ciencias Sociales, 1975). For a discussion of the *Catauro*'s "festivity," see Gustavo Pérez-Firmat, *Literature and Liminality* (Durham, N.C.: Duke Univ. Press, 1986) 93-108.

guabinas, hicoteas, patos y jutías" provokes a gentle, mocking smile "que rompe lo aparatoso, ilustre y trascendente en todas sus cerradas formas." This is accomplished, Vitier writes, "sin intención ni conciencia del autor, por la sola fuerza de los nombres."[46] In the series quoted from Vitier, Sarduy slips a word which does not appear in the original. Between Vitier's "aguacates" and "pitajayas," between the alligator pear that gives Lezama "el puré cotidiano de lo maravilloso incorporado" and the heady, nocturnal smell of the *Cactus grandiflorus,* Sarduy slyly inserts "siguapas," nocturnal bird of prey, also phantasm, apparition. In Sarduy's deliberate "error" lurks the subject, misquoter, inserter of words in someone else's text. One of the Narrators in *La Dolores* says that she disdains her origins, "Desprecia lo esencial, el lugar de su origen." The other one replies, "Calla estúpido. Lo esencial está entre la guanábana y el mango" (60), or between Vitier's "aguacates" and "pitajayas," for that matter, in the renewed possibility of inserting yet another term, the phantasmagoric, preying "siguapas."

To unhinge transcendence, the "power of names" supersedes authorial intention, and tricks all self-consciousness. In *De donde son los cantantes* Auxilio and Socorro have the formidable task of incarnating that power and of making it propel the narrative. The pair's journey through the Cuban countryside is a sustained reference not only to Martí's *Diario,* but to Vitier's reading of it. Vitier writes of "la intemperie cruda" (275), a peculiar sense of the outdoors in Martí's last notes; Mortal begins to decompose during his encounter with "lo descampado cubano" (126). *De donde*'s "la enumeración exhaustiva de los árboles" (125-126) corresponds to the "enumeración arbórea" (269) that Vitier signals in Martí, the poet's final desire to name "the meanest flower that blooms." Vitier begins his study with a discussion of the *Diary* of Columbus, as recorded by Las Casas, linking the Admiral's fascination with the island with Martí's own, and cites a famous phrase from the *Diary,* "vieron caer del cielo un maravilloso ramo de fuego en el mar" (20). When *De donde* describes

---

[46] *Escrito sobre un cuerpo* 69-70. Sarduy quotes from Cintio Vitier, *Lo cubano en la poesía* (1958; La Habana: Instituto del Libro, 1970) 38. Subsequent references to Vitier will be made in the text by page number in parenthesis.

Auxilio-Socorro's proximity to the islands, the same line from Columbus is quoted, with a footnote no less, *"Vimos un ramo de fuego caer sobre el mar"* (108). Vitier's concept of *lo cubano* is wide, and Sarduy can take what best suits his novel: "el desenfadado aparejamiento de palabras/ la sola fuerza de los nombres." In Vitier's summary "ornamento" is one of the values in his Cuban "constellation": "barroquismo frutal indiano, voluptuosidad, estilo del criollo, filigrana vegetal, *floreo* del danzón, realidad como arabesco sobre la nada, espiral del instante, adiós de la naturaleza o despedida del ser a sí mismo" (575). For Sarduy "reality" is a metaphysical category in a system which his textual practice contests. For him, it is writing that is Vitier's "arabesco sobre la nada, espiral del instante, adiós de la naturaleza o despedida del ser a sí mismo" (574). In Sarduy "la nada" may be a void, but it is a generating void.[47] As pointed out in *La ruta de Severo Sarduy,* the source of *lo cubano* is Vitier, not an essence, but a text. Quoting from it, the Sarduy subject surges where least expected, in a sustained, erratic allusive process. Yet he surges only to fade, crisscrossed by the power of names, "sabicú, guamá, roble, anoncillo" (126). He is Dolores in a Vegetalia Cicloide. He is Flor de Loto peeking behind the web woven by Auxilio and Socorro.

The fading subject comes to lodge in the parading figure of Mortal, in its "hinges," filled by Auxilio-Socorro: "Le rellenaban los intersticios de las articulaciones, Le abrigaban las bisagras" (141). The group moves through an urbanscape which could be taken from Burroughs's *Blade Runner,* "through a maze of derelict buildings"

---

[47] Méndez Rodenas alludes to this in her discussion of the "neobarroco" in *De donde:* "En el neobarroco esta esencia [of the classical sign, of mimetic literature] se sustituye por el centro vacío, ausente, de la Nada. En *De donde son los cantantes* la Nada se erige como categoría 'esencial,' y por lo tanto, suplanta al origen pleno que previamente originaba al signo representativo: la Cuba verídica, la cual definía al ser y a la historia" (107-108). This would place Sarduy's text on the side of a kind of nihilism erected as an essential category, as suggested by Barrenechea, p. 234, and corresponding to one of the possibilities outlined by Santi, the text as "the nihilism of a total fiction" (158). I have tried to suggest that Sarduy's text attempts to unravel such dualities, that "la nada" is a figure of absence, not an essence; it is a generating void, a post-modern cornucopia of the signifier. The novelty of Sarduy's "neobaroque" would therefore seem to hinge on its radical difference from the Baroque's metaphysical *desengaño.*

buildings" or from the film by the same name.[48] The setting is a phantasmagoric version of Havana at the turn of the century, the twenty-first that is, the Almendares filled with dying fish. Auxilio and Socorro print Mortal's name on their bodies, nearly completing the transformation of decaying body into legible text. The end is a cliffhanger, a cartoon reel spun loose from the turning wheel of a projector, flapping merrily. Auxilio and Socorro do reappear in *Cobra*, "Más que textuales apergaminadas y retóricas," already part of a "Sarduy" tradition, and in *Escrito sobre un cuerpo*, discussing Lezama's greatness; in Havana?, asks Socorro: "¡No hija, de la HISTORIA!"[49] In *Maitreya*, they are "Las tanatoprácticas," cutting up the Master's cadaver, "Siguiendo con esmero las articulaciones,"[50] already plotting his, and their, rebirth. One may recall the hinged body of Mortal-Christ, Barthes's cadaverous literature, Lacan's cadaveric signifier, and Whitman's "cadaverous meaning." As in a New Orleans funeral, however, what matters most in Sarduy is not the drive toward death but the dancing jig punctuating it. Auxilio and Socorro, death handlers, are nevertheless always on the rebound; their regression, like that of Peirce's interpretants, is infinite. In *Colibrí*, they resurface as ineluctable attendants, "las *bonitas de un lado*," "regulares como las figurillas grotescas que salen de un reloj."[51] They are part of a semiotic process, not pawns in a cause-effect relationship; the end of their journey is not as ominous as it is conventional. In Peirce's pragmatic semiotics, "the acquisition of habits is the ultimate logical interpretant of intellectual signs."[52] Criticism may be such a habit, bad habit, or pragmatic "logical interpretant," not ultimate one would hope, perhaps regressive.

The final *Nota*, balancing at the edge of the novel says that "Este hombre es el mismo" (152), suggesting the place of a subject that cannot be reduced to Auxilio's materialism, nor to Socorro's

---

[48] *Blade Runner (a movie)* (Berkeley: Blue Wind, 1979) n.p. Except for a futuristic, urban seeting, Burroughs's "script" bears little resemblance to the film which nevertheless uses the same title. The film was directed by Ridley Scott, Warner Brothers, 1982.

[49] *Cobra* (Buenos Aires: Sudamericana, 1974) 91; *Escrito sobre un cuerpo* 83.

[50] (Barcelona: Barral, 1978) 73-74.

[51] (Barcelona: Argos Vergara, 1984) 63, 69.

[52] John J. Fitzgerald, *Peirce's Theory of Signs as Foundation for Pragmatism* (The Hague: Mouton, 1967) 172.

transcedence; the subject is neither transcendental ego, an existential Other, nor pure signifying materialism associated with a "closed" text. The coming around of the subject replays such contrasts, without pretending to solve them. The linearity of the story, Borges's "adventure" is not banished; its "artificiality," distant from the pale affirmations of the first person, of all persons, from the ironic silliness of all narrative voices, serves as the setting for another story, the intermittent tale of the dethroned fool who wears the crown/wig in the topsy-turvy world of the last section. Auxilio and Socorro's triadic fantasies guarantee the economy of fiction, two for the price of (an absent) one; as they move, they do the *pasodoble,* while picking up the pieces of Mortal "con amor," for Mortal as subject is the writer/reader, not an entity, but a process. Inscribed as productivity in the text, he is the excentric dervish whose turnings do not define a circle, but who aims to surface on the side of the other, provisional, desired, center of an ellipse: "entonces la cadena deja caer al sujeto de su lugar único, lo *desorbita,* y éste viene a situarse, como un reverso de su brillo, en la noche del centro segundo."[53]

---

[53] Severo Sarduy, *Barroco* (Buenos Aires: Sudamericana, 1974) 78.

11
Character, author, and subject

1. MODELS OF CHARACTERIZATION: TEXTUALITY AND BIOGRAPHICAL ALIBI

As an introduction to a discussion of characterization and subjectivity in *De donde son los cantantes,* it will be useful to review some models of characterization, by way of establishing contrasts with Sarduy's novel. Rather than "model," one may refer to "aspects" or "features" of characterization – features of characterization associated with these names: Forster, Kristeva, Bakhtin, Barthes, Unamuno. Readers familiar with this territory may adjourn to the following section, which deals with characterization in *De donde son los cantantes.*

If the place of the subject is intermittently held by a signifier, it may be said that in a narrative, through the actions of the characters, a wearing down of the traditional, "round" character, whose ultimate signified would be "life," is played out. Characterization then becomes a function of a subjective process, whose goal is the recasting of an absent visage into a legible persona. It may be said that such a recasting is characteristic of any writing enterprise, for even in the most realistic of tales what the text gives us is never the "proper" image of character or author, but at best the photographic negative of that image, altered in the relays of language. However, the relationship between fictional personae and their maker is radically dramatized in *De donde son los cantantes.* Pronouns and proper names constantly subvert biographical alibi, defining the text as the space of a hunt, a "cruise," in which a virtual reader is ever pursued. To read is to accept a role, the temporary role of one whose presence the characters demand, whose absence structures their search.

Sarduy's emphasis on the activity of writing as the deferment of a biographical alibi, his inscribed "tampering" with the logic of the realistic narrative transform the narrative from a record left by an author into a subjective process requiring a peculiar kind of participation. Julia Kristeva has suggested that when an author tries to efface himself in the process of narration, he may appear as a zero degree of the "sujet de l'énonciation," an absent author who yields his role to a third person, the character. Or the author as "sujet de l'énoncé" and "sujet de l'énonciation," as the subject in the tale and subject of the telling, may coincide in the use of the first person, which marks the moment of discourse. In a third case, the author may coincide with the reader in the use of the second person. If the author uses all of these modes, as does Sarduy, the novel becomes an anatomy of writing, revealing the "mise en scène" of the book's "dialogic structure."[1] The text is the "productivity" or the process where a fundamental questioning of writing unfolds. Writing presents a theatrical space where the *I* "plays itself," "a space where *I* "multiplies," where it wears itself out. The first person is an actor calling out to a spectator, but neither the *I*, nor the spectator, is privileged in the theatrical space of writing (351). When writing becomes productivity, the first person yields its claim to authorial power and undermines the anthropomorphic conceit which may invest an author with the marks of authority and humanity all at once. In *De donde son los cantantes*, the notion of a total body of the author, removed from his work, in a myth of vitality that separates him from it as body from soul, is replaced by the notion of the text as a different sort of "place," a reconstituted "body" to which the writing subject lays claim in the exchange that s/he triggers.

In Sarduy's textual practice, the first person no longer relies on the duality between the "body" and "language." In fact, the concept of "person" yields to that of "signifying body," a *corpus*. The text as productivity aims to supersede the split between body and soul, to rescue the banished body, not in its ideal totality but as fragment, the bits and pieces gathered by Auxilio-Socorro at the end of *De donde son los cantantes*. The

---

[1] *Sémeiotikè: Recherches pour une sémanalyse* (Paris: Seuil, 1969) 170-171. Subsequent consecutive references in the text by page number in parenthesis.

CHARACTER, AUTHOR, AND SUBJECT

work of the text is the "sacrificial pillar" where the body is destroyed, so that in its absence the text may yield its load, the pleasure of textual production, which is not merely writing, but must encompass the always potential, and desired, act of reading. The subject in the text is neither psychological nor clinical; it is a by-product of writing, where the notion of "body," as the narcissistic "temple" of a metaphysical humanism, yields to the concept of *corpus,* the place where the productivity of the text is inscribed (351-352). Textual productivity is not the romantic toil of creation; it is wed to the myth of the pleasure of the economy of language, the only vehicle of desire. The *I* of the author and the narcissistic, metaphysical subject it implies, are undone, reborn as textual particles, parts of a body of signs that define an erotic exchange, not an exchange between bodies, but the sharing of a semiotic legacy in the symbolic order of language. It is an alteration of the dichotomy soul/body, on which depends the romantic division between "language as expression" and "body as vital and inaccessible." The "body" finds its only definition in the work of language, in the making of the text. As a reader, one may look for the narrative consequences of the "splitting" of the subject, divided through the language that defines him/her, his biographical self never coinciding with an anthropomorphic plenitude, but eternally shattered in the symbolic topography of language.

In *De donde son los cantantes,* the relationship of the subject, fundamentally split by his initiation into language, dispersed at the level of narrative among "floating" pronouns, unfolds in a space which has been frequently described as a "theatrical" space. The theatricality of Sarduy's novel is a prelude to Barthes's quasi-autobiographical travel essay, *L'Empire des signes,* whose authorial first person is shown to be the floating signifier never centered on the one who writes, ever redefined in terms of the language that envelops it. If the first person pronoun in defined in terms of the instances in which it is found, Barthes dramatizes this functional use of the pronoun as an empty mark only to be filled by its user, and throws his own name into the game, withdrawing it from the alibi which ties it to the man and making it instead a sign that can only be understood in terms of the plurality of signs found in the text. In Barthes's essay, the idea of a body corresponding to the proper name yields to that of a body coded in the text. His "hero" is shattered, masked by a series of pronouns, reduced to legible gestures.

The distinction between two kinds of authorial bodies is discussed in Kristeva's early work, *Le texte du roman*.[2] A study of the fifteenth century work *Jehan de Saintré,* Kristeva's essay restates the opposition between two authorial models, and correlatively between the novel as literature on the one hand, and the notion of textuality as productivity on the other. The traditional novel's representational conceit presupposes an author anterior to the text, and a reader posterior to it. Upholding the value of its own representation, of its own "world," the novel rests on two separate bodies, both paradoxically separated as independent entities. The novel presupposes a writing subject who expresses meaning through it. Thus the representational novel rests on Saussure's fundamental splitting of the sign, which has allowed the marketing of transcendence characteristic of the genre. Following Lacan's use of the Saussurean sign, in a definition of the text as productivity, the text gives up representation to become the inscription of its own production. Representation in the novel is associated with the hegemony of the classic sign; textuality, on the other hand, emulating the space of the carnival, does not depend on the transcendence of that which is before or after its production. Kristeva contrasts the idea of story associated with the novel and that of working activity associated with the text. The text as productivity works "against the grain" of the novel as the individual's adventure. *Le texte du roman* develops the opposition between two kinds of authors, distinguishing between the etymologically related words, "acteur" and "auteur." The "actor" in a narrative is the rhetorical subject, manifested for example through different pronouns, while the "author" of a novel is the literary subject, an extratextual, though no less reconstituted, marketable persona founded on the idea of the individual's body, on its "reality."

In *Jehan de Saintré* the first person pronoun does not refer to a specific person; it is "an empty I," a shifter signalling the moment of discourse, (99). The actor-agent, a rhetorical subject,

---

[2] *Le texte du roman* (Paris: Mouton, 1970). Subsequent consecutive references in the text by page number in parenthesis.

is the subject of the signifier, defined by its display. By contrast, the notion of "author," of the literary, biographical subject depends on the signified. Such an author may lay claim to a corporeity prior to the text. This literary, biographical author, characteristic of the realistic novel, is "anterior to writing," bound to an idea that precedes the word. This "transcendental subject" appears as a double of the author, who is in turn distanced from the narrative enunciation itself. When this "transcendental" subject uses the first person the text becomes literature, a product marketed in a particular economy. If the epic may be said to have had no author, no literary author, the appearance of the novel coincides with the transformation of "actor" into "author." This passage from the functional first person of an actor-agent to an "I" capable of being associated with a human being marks the birth of the kind of novel in which an individual with a biography becomes the maker of a representation (100-101).

De donde son los cantantes marks a reverse passage, from the notion of "author" to that of "actor-agent," the transformation of the masterful, quasi-biographical first person of the author into a functional, textual first person. The novel's plurality of narrative techniques brings the subjectivity of the author into the play of pronominal positions. It aims to unseat the biographical author, to transform the text into bio-graphy. From the notion of the unity of the body which backs up the author of the representational novel, the novel moves toward a definition of a plural textual body, where characters are no longer at the service of that author's implicit glorification, but rather dramatize his demise, his textual undoing.

Writing about character, Barthes refers to the powerful convention, richly developed by the realistic novel, that immediately identifies a fictional hero with the human being that he might have been or might be, as if the narrative were determined at a referential level, confusing "character" as "narrative agent" with "character" as an ethical quality of a human being.[3] Expressing unease with the terminology associated with traditional characterization, Barthes defines character, as a "paper creature," echoing

---

[3] Roland Barthes, "Introduction à l'analyse structurale des récits," *Communications* 8 (1966): 19.

Genette's desire for a more "neutral" term, which would dissociate the narrative agent from "unduly" human characteristics.[4]

Anticipating Genette's attempt to define character as narrative agent and Barthes's positing of character as a "paper creature," E. M. Forster discusses characterization under the heading "People" in *Aspects of the novel*. Although granting the possibility of future developments in fictional characterization, Forster begins by restating the formula which equates human beings with the actors in a narrative. "The actors in a story," writes Forster, "are, or pretend to be, human beings."[5] The argument hinges on the phrase "pretend to be," for Forster recognizes that characters in a novel are in fact not human beings. He identifies a character as a "word-mass," composed of names, descriptions of behavior, dialogue. The opposition between human beings and the fictional entities which attempt to represent them in the novel leads Forster into making the useful distinction between *"homo sapiens,"* and an "allied species," called *"homo fictus"* (55). Forster's *homo fictus* coincides with Unamuno's "criatura de ficción";[6] however, though both models are suggestive antecedents for Sarduy's approach to characterization, they rest on radically different presuppositions.

For Forster and Unamuno, the "reality" of the fictional character depends on the independence, on the self-sufficiency of the work of art, and correlatively on the separation between life and art. Forster's metaphysical load refers to "human psychology," which is rendered more intelligible by art. Although, referring to his well-known distinction between "flat" and "round" characters, he says that "there may be more in flatness than the severer critics admit," his test for a good fiction is the creation of round characters – "life within the pages of a book" (78). Unamuno adds to this psychology of "depth," of a "secret life," his own existential rethinking of Christianity. For him the independent reader is "autor de ti mismo." For both Unamuno and Forster, the fictional quality of a character, is the counterpart of the individual's humanity. From opposites sides of the ring,

---

[4] *Figures III* (Paris: Seuil, 1972) 252n.
[5] *Aspects of the Novel* (New York: Harcourt, Brace, & World, 1927) 44. Subsequent page references in the text in parenthesis.
[6] *Cómo se hace una novela* (1926; Madrid: Alianza, 1978) 144.

Forster and Unamuno call for a dialogic rapport among characters, but the rules of their game do not alter the unity of the individual, a unity shaken by their modernist irony, but holding out after all. In *De donde son los cantantes,* the boundaries between the opposites defined by Unamuno and Forster begin to give way, in order to open a dialogic space which overflows Bakhtin's idealism, to define an ongoing subjectivity traced in writing, inseparable from it.

While admitting that it is the shift in "view-point" of the author in relation to his characters that gives the novel its unique "right to intermittent knowledge," Forster values the creation of character above what he calls the exploration of the novelist's own mind. Referring to Gide's *Les Faux Monnayeurs,* he writes, "The novelist who betrays too much interest in his own method, can never be more than interesting; he has given up the creation of character and summoned us to help analyse his own mind, and a heavy drop in the emotional thermometer results" (80). By contrast to Forster's ultimately representational aesthetics, a work such as *De donde son los cantantes* exploits to the fullest the writer's "right to intermittent knowledge" by bringing into the foreground the relationship of the writer to the text, and by making the novel not a means to render reality, inner or outer, but rather by making the text a meditation on the means through which a shared reality is constituted. The text is mimetic only inasmuch as it puts forth the terms of such a medi(t)ation.

Forster's "secret life," the interiority which has gone hand in hand with modern literature, is a limited literary effect. With Freud, and Lacan's emphasis on the split of the subject, the fiction of an internal voice gives way to the subject's radical exteriority, his heteronomous status in relation to language. In *De donde son los cantantes,* the emphasis is on the exteriority of the individual in relation to language, on the fact that his "secret life" is no secret, but rather a territory common to all. In such a text, characterization is redefined, no longer in terms of "people," Forster's heading, but in terms of the "wordmasses" to which he also refers.

The contemporary text establishes between narrator and characters a variable, or "floating," relation, a pronominal spin corresponding to an unfettered logic, to a more complex idea of the personality.⁷ Such a complex idea of personality is correlative to a view of the unconscious as language, a boundless reserve which informs the individual's every move, which tailors his desire. If the subject ceases to be the source of an a priori plenitude to invest himself in language, trafficking in his own state of "absence," the producer of a text can barely suggest a biographical presence in the fictional visages of his characters.

De donde son los cantantes dramatizes the difficulty of locating in a text what Barthes calls "the place of the subject" among the characters, "la place du sujet dans toute matrice actancielle." The reading of such a text involves the staking out of the territory where the subject of a narrative, its "hero," lurks. The place of Barthes's plural "hero" may be read in the pronouns used, in the actions of the characters. Wherever it appears, even in notes, Sarduy's first person partakes of the complex, Proustean model in which author, narrator, and hero may be a single "persona" but not the same "person." Discussing Proust's "casual" mention of the name "Marcel," in *A la recherche,* Gérard Genette writes that the hegemony of the Proustean first person and the casual mention of the proper name in the text do not signal a comfortable truce with the "subjectivity" of the self; on the contrary, what is indicated is the arduous experience of the self marked by distance and excentricity – "un rapport à soi vécu comme (légère distance) et décentrement."⁸

In the Japan visited by Barthes, the strangeness of the language which surrounds the writer makes him keenly aware of such an "off-centering" of the self, an experience which is not marked by pathos or nostalgia, but rather by the kind of sudden enlightenment associated with Zen. In *L'Empire des signes,* "Japan" is defined as a fiction no less willful than that which constitutes the author. "Japan" is the writer's fantasy, which is only "compromised" in "the signs of literature,"⁹ in its passage from fantasy to

---

⁷ Foreshadowed by Borges in "La nadería de la personalidad," *Inquisiciones* (Buenos Aires: Proa, 1925).
⁸ *Figures III* 256.
⁹ *L'Empire des signes* (Geneva: Skira, 1970) 9. Subsequent references in the text by page number in parenthesis.

readable surface. The movements of the writer among the "pure signifiers" of the radically foreign language which "envelops" him produces a "slight vertigo," which carries him along, emptying him of "meaning": "je vis dans l'interstice, débarrassé de tout sens plein" (18). Emptiness and lack of meaning may be associated with the dialectics of existential anguish, but Barthes stresses that the experience he describes is far from solemn ("nullement solennel"). The radical experience of language as pure signifier is called "un séisme," a shake-up of the subject, of his way of knowing – something which "fait vaciller la connaissance, le sujet" (11). In Sarduy, the subject's "vacillation" is even less solemn, for "vaciller," becomes "vacilar," to vacilate and to raise Cain, Sarduy's own scriptural "vacilón," the Caribbean hoedown of *De donde son los cantantes*.

The experience of the subject described by Barthes is developed in his commentaries on the traditional Japanese theatre of dolls or Bunraku. *De donde* also uses theatrical settings as the scene of the subject's comedy of terrors, a topos carried on in *Cobra*'s "Teatro lírico de muñecas,"[10] in the pageantry of the Tibetan monks in *Maitreya*, in the antics in *Colibrí*'s "La Casona." In *L'Empire des signes*, the puppets and their handlers in Bunraku dramatize a process of characterization akin to Sarduy's own.

Associated in its development and form with Kabuki theatre, Bunraku, the puppet theatre of Japan, takes its present name from that of a puppeteer-producer who restored its popularity in the nineteenth century. Its development may be traced to a sixteenth century combination of popular puppet theatre, recitations accompanied by musical instruments, and other aspects of Japanese performing arts.[11] What is distinctive about the Bunraku is the "complete division of labor, into visual and aural elements."[12] The spectacle is composed of three elements: the approximately one-third human size puppets, elaborately costumed, the main ones having mechanisms which move mouth and eyebrows; the visible operators, since the eighteenth century three for most

---

[10] See González Echevarría, *Relecturas* 137-138.

[11] Peter Arnott, *The Theatre of Japan* (New York: St. Martin's Press, 1969) 186-187.

[12] Toshio Kawatake, *A History of Japanese Theater* II (Japan: Kokusai Bunka Shinkokai [Japan Cultural Society], 1971) 16.

figures, one being the master who moves the head and right arm; the other two, his assistants, who move the other arm and the legs or dress; finally, the chanter or chanters, accompanied by musicians, who present the story, their voice synchronized in mood and tone to the actions of the dolls.

Scholars writing for a Western audience on the art of the Japanese puppet theatre invariably apologize for the fact that the manipulators are visible. By contrast, Barthes sees the three activities that compose Bunraku as fundamental to the spectacle, three modes of "writing," defined as an activity where the process of producing meaning is not veiled, but rather displayed. What Barthes admires in Bunraku and in Japanese culture in general is the open display of the techniques through which a given effect is achieved. The Japanese cook, to cite another example from *L'Empire des signes*, is not in the hidden, forbidden kitchen of traditional Western cuisine, which produces heavily glazed wonders; he is in the midst of the diners, displaying his mastery and involving them in it at the same time. In Bunraku theatre, the use of three separate, equally important planes of operation allows for a combination of art and craft, which traditional Western theatre has masked. The voices of the Bunraku chorus express emotion, "toute la cuisine de l'émotion," but they play a limited role, consciously detached from the gesture of the doll, its most rending pathos given according to a fixed code, "le code même du débordement" (69). The dolls present the emotive gestures, while the operators are openly seen as the actors, in the functional sense, behind their movements. The simultaneous presentation of the three activities precludes the mystification of the voice as unique means of expression or of the operators as hidden causes.

In the Western actor, the voice is said to be expression of an interior state, and the hidden operators of the Western puppet are the human causes of its erratic movements. Barthes relates this causality to the idea of the human soul and of God, which is at the base of traditional characterization in literature, the kind that values the "roundness" or the psychological complexity or "depth" of a fictional character. The Western actor lends to the character he is portraying the "alibi" of unity suggested by his/her body, "l'alibi d'une unité organique, celle de la 'vie'" (79). Beneath this illusory unity, the actor hides the division of his own body, composed in fact not as a unit but as separate parts: voice, look, gestures. It is this division which the Western puppet caricatures in its spastic movements, "projection décomposée des gestes du corps." The puppet appears ridiculous because, animated by an unseen agent and reproducing but a disjointed part of a man's movement, it mocks as it asserts all at once the concept of the body as organic unity and of the soul as internal directing cause. The Bunraku marionette and its visible operators, on the other hand, do not imitate the human body in its imagined anthropomorphic totality. The Bunraku puppet sidesteps the duality "animate/inanimate," and in so doing refuses the idea of soul which "hides" behind all *"animation"* of matter (81).

In *L'Empire des signes,* the Japanese doll abolishes the "metaphysical link" between the Western dualities of soul/body, cause/effect, Creator/creatures (84). Correlatively, it undermines the Saussurean body/soul metaphor as one of the models of the signifier/signified. In Barthes's excentric "reading" of Japanese culture, the signifier dominates while the effects of the signified are, if not exiled, suspended, deferred. As a subject writing on Japan, Barthes records not only a cultural landscape, but also the transformation of the writing subject inserted in a new, radically foreign language. A Japanese friend complained that Barthes's Japan is almost pure fantasy, and she is right; a book about Japan is written by Barthes, but what I read is not "Japan" but a Barthes "japonisé."

In Sarduy's works, the Japanese theatre discussed by Barthes becomes a recurring topos for the relationship author/character. Like the manipulators of the Bunraku dolls, the author in Sarduy takes on an operational, a readable role. The division of labor that separates "visual" and "aural" elements in the Bunraku is not glossed over, but deliberately marked, and in the boundaries of those divisions, the subject is installed, his blank "face" open to a reading. If Barthes writing of Japan becomes a Barthes "japonisé," when Sarduy writes of Cuba in Paris, what is his textual visage? If the text supplants "la Cuba histórica" with "una Cuba enmascarada,"[13] it also supplants Sarduy, not with a Sarduy "afrancesado," perhaps with a Sarduy "cubanisé."

---

[13] Méndez Rodenas 34.

By contrast to the illusory unity of the biographical author, Genette's "signataire," the subject in the text becomes a different kind of hero, one with a fragmented, kaleidoscopic visage, a moving, changing subject, who lodges in a multiplicity of grammatical persons, cut up, stretched, like the dolls in *Cobra,* in the process of enunciation. Sarduy's "plural" hero harks back to the work of Bakhtin, introduced in France with *La Poétique de Dostoievski.* In the introduction to Bakhtin's concept of the polyphonic novel, Julia Kristeva refers to the character's role as a "discursive position" available to the writer, a way of multiplying his first person into a series of grammatical persons which signal the "dialogic" quality of the novel.[14] Bakhtin sees in Dostoevsky, "a radical alteration of the author's position," and comments on the opposition between biographical versus textual subject. Like the "hero" in *De donde son los cantantes,* the Dostoevskian hero overflows the limits of the biographical subject; he cannot be "'incarnated'" as such a subject.[15]

The waning of the biographical subject as the alibi of the characters in a text, and the affirmation of the dialogic quality of the writer's production coincide with the banishment of what Bakhtin calls "le serieux monologique" (219). In narrative, "serious monologue" depends on an "idealism," which Bakhtin seeks to undermine, a limited cognitive practice similar to the tradi-

---

[14] "Une poétique ruinée", *La Poétique de Dostoievski,* trans. Isabelle Kolitcheff (Paris: Seuil, 1970) 15.

[15] I use the French rather than the English translation, *Problems of Dostoevsky's Poetics,* trans. R. W. Rotsel (U.S.A.: Ardis, 1973) because its terminology, which is to say its bias, is better suited to a reading of Sarduy. The two versions show certain discrepancies which one may note in passing. Compare for example the following passages: "In this sense Dostoevsky's hero is not, and cannot be, concretely embodied and dream of joining in a normal-life plot (normal nyi zhiznennyi siuzhet)," trans. Rotsel (83). In French: "Le héros de Dostoïevski, lui, ne se prête pas à une telle 'incarnation.' Il est incapable de tenir dans un sujet biographique normal; au contraire: tous ses efforts pour 's'incarner' restent vains," trans. Kolitcheff (145). The French suggests that the Dostoevskian "hero" overflows the limits of a "normal biographical subject," which seems overly explicatory; on the other hand, the English seems awkward, particularly in its parenthetical inclusion of the transliterated Russian phrase. Emir Rodríguez Monegal mentions the ambiguities of the translations, already noted in Kristeva's introduction. Significantly, it seems that even Bakhtin's name does not escape the carnivalization proposed by his books: Bakhtine, Bajtín, Bactin. See Rodríguez Monegal, "Carnaval/ Antropofagia/ Parodia," *Revista Iberoamericana* 44 (1979): 401-412.

tional relationship between the "master" and his pupils, those who have the truth teaching it to those who do not have it (122). The discourse of the university, marked by the "serieux monologique," contrasts with the tradition of "carnivalized literature." In *De donde son los cantantes,* a "carnivalized" conception of character is correlative to the novel's rewriting of "authority," to its undermining of the "idealism" on which Bakhtin's "serieux monologique" is founded. However, the ultimate dominance of the subject is not questioned in Bakhtin, while the dialogic quality of *De donde son los cantantes* depends on such a questioning. The "carnivalization" in Sarduy's text is not merely thematical or limited to a plurality of narrative voices; it is a subjective process which unravels the logic of theme, characterization, and narrative voice, a shake up of the house of fiction, a questioning of its possibilities and its limitations.

Bakhtin defines "carnivalized" literature as that which has received directly or indirectly the influence of certain aspects of the folklore of the ancient or medieval carnival (152). Such a literature, lacking in epic or tragic distance, usually describes contemporary events. It renounces a "monostyle" and adopts a plurality of styles and of "voices," mixing different kinds of genres; the author does not remain fixed on anyone point of view, but shifts as the text progresses (152-153). The festival associated with the actual carnival does not separate actors and spectators; likewise, the literature of the carnival would blur the distinction between author and reader, active producer and passive receiver. It privileges the text as the place of a non-hierarchical exchange; it would be teaching without didacticism, love without possession. Bakhtin refers to the Renaissance carnival, which has ceased to provoke a carnivalesque situation in European culture. What is to be retained of the carnival as model is not its referential validity, but its affirmation of marginality, its questioning of a logocentric tradition.

In the context of Latin American culture, the carnival retains its validity as a model; even if it did not, or when it no longer does, other cultural manifestations duplicate and will duplicate carnivalesque situations, among them the Cuban tradition of *santería,* and in literature, the work of Borges, Lezama, Jorge Amado, and Sarduy.[16] The carnivalesque in Sarduy is not only suggested in the use of yoruba elements, particularly in *La Dolores Rondón*,[17] but also corresponds to his peculiar transformations of the continental theories of the subject and the realm of fiction to which he has access – transformations because the references to such theories in his work do not constitute a theoretical framework, but a textual one, which means that the novel "resists" in turn a theoretical reading, only yielding, perhaps to a dialogic one.

The carnivalized text reverses the usually accepted order of things. It mixes the sacred and the profane, the high and the low, the blessing and the curse, the young and the old, the sublime and the insignificant, the wise and the stupid (171). Bakhtin describes certain acts typical of the carnival, such as the "enthronement" of the fool and the correlative destitution of the king, and finds in this act what is most characteristic of the carnivalesque perception of the world: the pathos of decadence and revival, of death and rebirth (172). It is this process, not a specific change itself, which is celebrated in the carnival, the transformation of rag into banner, of ordure into sparkle. *La Entrada de Cristo en La Habana* may be read as the rewriting of the Cuban Revolution as carnival, as *comparsa,* an oblique celebration of the revolutionary event as the fleeting suspension of history.

The classic side of the satiric element in *De donde son los cantantes* is neither Juvenalian nor Horatian; its roots may be traceable to the Greek cynic Menippus, discussed by Bakhtin as paradigm of carnivalized literature. Menippean satire is a changing, supple form, not constrained by the idea of story or plot. It does not claim to hold to an esthetics of verisimilitude, but rather exploits the thematic possibilities of a plural vision. In this genre, story, plot and character are bent or sacrificed in favor of the themes that concern the author (158-160). In the Menippean satire, genres are mixed; all sorts of sudden transformations take place, deaths and instant resurrections, falls and rises, in short, all forms of violent contrasts. In Menippean satire, the character loses its anthropomorphic unity, its ideological or moral "monism"; it stops coinciding with a fixed model, becoming part of a

---

[16] Rodríguez Monegal 408.
[17] See Justo Ulloa, "Contenido y forma yoruba en 'La Dolores Rondón' de Severo Sarduy," *Homenaje a Lydia Cabrera* 241-250.

dialogue that requires the constant presence of doubles. Anything that would upset an established order, a code of conduct or etiquette, including the use of "good" language, is embraced by the carnivalized genre (162-164).

De donde son los cantantes may not share "the essence of the genre," as defined by Bakhtin, nor is it a satire in the sense described by Frye, a combination of "fantasy and morality" with "stylized" characters.[18] What Sarduy's novel does share with the classic genre is its insistence on the subject's signalling that the "truth" of the world is a fictional act, that its truth does not depend on imitation, of the world or of a historical model, but on inscription.[19] The kind of tradition of opposition in which Sarduy's work participates is not merely the anti-bourgeois stance of the writer whose project is a resentful attack on a society that defuses such an attack the moment it is made. Rather, Sarduy's work reveals an awareness of the limitations of literary language in contesting the givens of a culture. In La Dolores Rondón it is the two ridiculous "Narradores" who carry on the debate concerning the value of the word, as if such debates were doomed from the start. What Sarduy's work combats is the reduction of the writing project to "le serieux monologique" described by Bakhtin; the writing project affirms plurality and seeks to define a dialogic space, akin to the carnival in that it temporarily lifts the accepted restrictions of the day-to-day world.

The concepts of "waste" and "replacement" used by Bakhtin to describe the carnivalesque worldview have an echo in a model of language implicit in De donde son los cantantes. The Peircean/Lacanian model of the sign as a a series of "interpreters" or "signifiers" never fixed on the pursued object and never allowing the subject to break the chain to affirm an illusory individual unity corresponds to Bakhtin's definition of a carnivalesque worldview whose common denominators are precisely displacement, plurality, replacement, contrast, all manifest in the polyphonic novel's shattering of the author/man, himself the mythic product of language, set aside, put in its place, circumscribed. The

---

[18] *Anatomy of Criticism* (Princeton, N.J.: Princeton University Press, 1957) 309-312.

[19] Lía Schwartz Lerner, "En torno a la enunciación en la sátira: los casos de *El Crótalon* y los *Sueños* de Quevedo," *Lexis* 9 (1985): 209-227.

novel avoids a monologic discourse and undermines the hierarchy author/ character/reader. It stages a plural vision which flees the fixed, the finished, the monographic. Its emphasis on the dominance of a plurality of signifiers replays Bakhtin's "intense" dialogic activity, at the same time superseding his transcendental subject with another "made up" of/in that very "waste," that "replacement."

The dialogic activity demanded of the writer by his plural, carnivalesque vision makes of the characters moving entities, pieces of various narrative instances, not nomenclaturally framed, "three-dimensional" unities. In Sarduy's novel, any claim to authority, above all the author's, is ridiculed, while the characters have as much to do with advancing a narrative thread as with signalling the writing activity as the novel's desired referent, writing as the oblique reflection of a plurality grounded on displacement and substitution, qualities of the sign which must inform the work of the writing subject.

The deferral of the body of the author as biographical alibi involves neither nihilism nor the inconsequential, punning playfulness which tags the product of writing as another prized commodity in the waning days of capitalism; rather, it signals the coming of the text as the record of an exchange, a controlled onsography which overflows the boundaries of the anthropomorphic ideal, a cultural product passing off as natural prodigy. The waning of the author is the beginning of writing, not as the expression of an absent voice, but as the mark of a potential complicity.

2. CHARACTERIZATION AND THE ELIDED SUBJECT

In *De donde son los cantantes,* the mocking of the authorial personas in the text may be said to correspond to another characteristic process: the deferral of the writing subject, who is nowhere in the text, yet is everywhere, in the interstices of the letter, as if the writing subject lurked in the nooks and crevices of the text, the record of a sustained effort to refract and transform a conventional authorial mask in the legible realm of the letter, an effort to overthrow what Julián del Casal called, citing DeQuincey, *"la tiranía del rostro humano."*[1]

In Sarduy's novel, the sustained contrast between a plurality of signifiers and an ever deferred signified, between the text as display of signifiers and the signified as the illusory finality of meaning, corresponds to the oppositions between a plurality of characters and authorial voices and a deferred writing subject, barred from the traditional accesses to the text: narrative voice, implicit authority etc., a subject who nevertheless surfaces in unexpected places. Formally, at the level of narrative, characterization dramatizes such contrasts, which ultimately dissolve in a process of display/displacement that overrides all opposites. As the space of an elusive subjectivity, the text exploits the multiplicity of discursive positions allowed by the narrative. The name of the signer, Severo Sarduy, remains in the periphery of the text, and the idea of his body is shattered to allow the writing process the privilege of becoming the metaphor of a readable corpus. What is at stake is the destruction of a model of the individual

---

[1] *Prosas,* 3 vols. (La Habana: Consejo Nacional de Cultura, 1963) 2: 119.

associated with an entity aloof from the text, addressing a reader secure in the illusion of his/her own body. The process of the text, its work, its writing and reading, inscribes a subjectivity defined as an ongoing commerce, an exchange held to the letter, to its limitations and its possibilities.

It is a not a question in *De donde son los cantantes* of allowing the characters in the narrative to become "masks," Unamuno's "criatura de ficción" or Forster's *homo fictus,* for an authorial voice winking in complicity at the reader. Such a device leaves the power of the authorial persona intact without radically breaking from a rich narrative tradition of anthropomorphism and verisimilitude. The "novelty" of Sarduy's work lies in its extravagant attempts to subvert such a tradition, to dwell in the shattering immanence of the letter. In Sarduy's novel, the character is a name, or names, or a pronoun, around which cluster a series of discourses which compose an illusory unity. The character is the meeting place of narrative and discursive structures, of the grammatical and the semantic components of the text.[2]

The character is the vehicle for action and the carrier of themes associated with its presence in the text. In the polyphonic text, there is no hierarchy of narrative voices; all contribute to the plurality of discourses. Characters, whether named "Auxilio" or "el autor," third persons, first persons, or any narrative "voice" merely insure the movement through the narrative of a writing subject whose place is constantly shifting. This uncertainty about the subject's place turns the novel into an anatomy of writing, and makes of the book the setting of a necessary dialogue.

The *Nota* at the end of *De donde son los cantantes* describes the opening *Curriculum Cubense* as the introduction of the characters. The *Curriculum* presents a sort of plan for the kind of characterization at work in this novel and in Sarduy's subsequent novels. The opening passage of the *Curriculum* is a description of Auxilio:

---

[2] A. J. Greimas, "Les actants, les acteurs, et les figures," *Sémiotique narrative et textuelle,* ed. Claude Chabrol (Paris: Larrouse, 1973) 55.

CHARACTER, AUTHOR, AND SUBJECT

> Plumas, sí, deliciosas plumas de azufre, río de plumas arrastrando cabezas de mármol, plumas en la cabeza, sombrero de plumas, colibríes y frambuesas; desde él caen hasta el suelo los cabellos anaranjados de Auxilio, lisos, de nylon, enlazados con cintas rosadas y campanitas, desde él a los lados de la cara, de las caderas, de las botas de piel de cebra, hasta el asfalto la cascada albina. (11)

An element of conventional characterization, the description of the character's hair, "los cabellos anaranjados de Auxilio," spills over into a description of a hat that swallows any anthropomorphic semblance. The anthropomorphic elements which compose the character's body, "la cara," "las caderas," are imbedded in a catalog which seems to issue "desde él," pronoun for Auxilio's hat, but also the "El," the absent one, which later surfaces in the narrative. Auxilio's very name conjures up her double before it appears: where there's Auxilio, Socorro cannot be far behind. Auxilio's paradigm, her next of kin, is Socorro; the two are instantly metonymic. They carry a semiotic legacy, in fact are pregnant with it in *La Entrada de Cristo en La Habana,* but their presence in the text is immediately symbolic. They insure that the text will move on as a signifying process. There are no areas of "non-sense" in *De donde son los cantantes;* every word in the novel fits in a symbolic pattern which is respected throughout. There are, however, recurring patterns in the text, which beyond authorial voice or point of view, or story, constitute what used to be called a "style," signs from the subject which define their own pattern, if not always readable, always symptomatic, generative of fragmentary patterns, which may be pieced together in a particular reading.

One such pattern, for example, is made up of rhetorical negation/affirmations, used by a narrative voice, by the characters, and by an authorial voice in the final *Nota. Junto al Río* begins with such a pattern, "Ni la luna, la perdiz..." (25), which is continued as follows: "Ella no palideció; lo estaba ya..." (25); "Hoy no irá al espectáculo. Espera..." (54); "no lo hemos perpetrado sino que..." (67); "No comen, no beben, ni juntan los entiesados párpados. Descifran..." (95); "No por estos pedruscos, oh labradores, ni por joya arqueológica alguna venimos, no; sino por los indicios de nuestro dueño" (95); "Ya los aparatos no los seguían a igual distancia, sino que..." (135); "La vida no comienza sino después de la muerte, la vida" (145); In the *Nota,* an authorial voices uses the *"excusatio propter infirmitatem,"* only to add "No la utilizo aquí (aunque esta denegación sea una de sus formas)" (153). Such a pattern cuts through characterization, narrative, and authorial voices; it constitutes a legible tic, whimsical first and last resorts, the healing strategies of a severed subject.[3]

The characters in *De donde* defy visualization. Auxilio's "Cabeza," "sombrero," "cabellos," "cara," "caderas," "botas" suggest fragmentation rather than unity, a skeletal framework covered with nylon "hair" and "feathers/pens," instantly transformed into a bird, "Y Auxilio rayada, pájaro indio detrás de la lluvia" (11). If anything, her mien recalls a Yoruba priest from an Ortiz nightmare. From the start, Auxilio is a "pájaro," bird and Cuban queen, transforming one aspect of characterization, namely description, into a constant signalling of the uncertainty of the signifier, of its drift. The word "pájaro" may be read in another pattern which begins with *Gestos* and is carried on to *Colibrí,* where the father warns "Sarduy" that if he continues to write, "jugando con fruticas de brilladera," he might be labeled as a "pájaro," (129).

González Echavarría identifies in *Gestos* a metaphoric/metonymic pattern centered on the word "pájaro." After the explosion in the electric plant, the shattered "vidrios vibrantes" rise "como pájaros." Subsequently, the dead "pájaros" fall heavily like "pedazos de hierro," which then turn into "flechas," flying off like birds. The explosion undoes a series of connections to suggest other links, "otros nexos que hacen por empatarse, por reconstituirse."[4] In *De donde son los cantantes,* the recurring "pájaro" explictly suggests that such connections constitute the surface structures of a lacunary subject, perhaps, like the General, "el pájaro pintor de Lacan que se quita sus plumas" (19). However,

---

[3] Roberto Echavarren "On Literariness," *Che Voui? In the Freudian Field: Journal of Psychoanalysis* 1.1 (1984): 90-91. Echavarren discusses Octave Mannoni, *Clefs pour l'imaginaire, l'autre scene* (Paris: Seuil, 1969), and writes that "Through the practice of negation," the subject has "the freedom to sever itself from what it literally is (although it doesn't coincide with what it imagines either). It becomes itself in an adventure of words, as a belief put into practice, that supposes negation as its functioning hinge."

[4] *La ruta de Severo Sarduy* 91.

the text is not a painting, and the subject not the colorful moulting bird but the participant in a different sort of economy.

The motif of the birds recurs throughout *Junto al Río*. Next to the Director, a bald, mysterious Chinese, naked, with a small, spiral phallus, "como un tornillito," proclaims – "El ser de los pájaros no es el timbre del trino, sino las plumas cayendo a cada muda," followed by a series of transformations: "muda" "despista dejando ojillos de culebra," "impostura," "doble ciego" (48), a replay of the metonymic sequence in *Gestos*. "Pájaros" is metonymy; it is also metaphor of a "subject" whose "being" is not only what is legible in a text, but what is lacunary, a subject who drops his feathers ("muda"), who tricks leaving false eyes ("despista dejando ojillos"), for the benefit of a "doble ciego," a sightless other, a mute reader. Yet for the sake of the reader, the symbolic order is maintained. Auxilio and Socorro must return. From the beginning, the first person as the possible emblem for the producer of the text is literally put in its place; it is a limited place which the plurality of the unfolding narrative, dominated by the semiotic pair, overflows. This and subsequent exchanges between a first person and the pair transform into fictional episode the familiar topos of contemporary textual theory: that the first person is but the temporary mark of the instance of discourse, that the "hero" of the text is not bound by grammatical persons, but is the subject of a process obliquely dramatized in the text.

Characterization becomes a process of layering the double entity Auxilio-Socorro. Beneath the river of hair, five layers of make-up, yielding only to a power drill, obliterate the face, where emotion has traditionally been written. Her face is full of holes, like the moon, "como la cara de la luna: llena de cráteres." In a crossfire of hyperbolic insults, Auxilio finally snaps, "Que te chupe la falla lacaniana. Que seas absorbida, desapercibida por inadvertida" (12). The subject lurks in Auxilio's insult, "desapercibida por inadvertida," a reference to the now almost accepted semantic overlapping of the two words, although "desapercibido" may be considered a "galicismo" when used in the place of "inadvertido." Alfredo Pabón, late Cuban professor and author of *Cuestiones lingüísticas y gramaticales* (1947), calls it a semantic "vice" among certain Cuban writers, "En este vicio incurren no pocos escritores y periodistas en Cuba, no obstante las críticas hechas por insignes gramáticos sobre esta incorrección."[5] Auxilio and Socorro, subjective agents, are privy to the arcana of Cuban linguistics. Auxilio's insult may allude to one of the subject's Gallic vices. More significantly, it may be said that the subject lurks in the overlapping of two traditionally incompatible signifiers which have come to refer to a third, shared term, "unnoticed." It is in such unexpected relays that the subject surfaces. The status of the subject is precisely to go "unnoticed," but he surges in the errant pairing of semantic siblings, "desapercibida/inadvertida," Auxilio/Socorro.

As the narrative unfolds, Auxilio and Socorro blend into one character, two textual participants with a common role. They are "simétricas," walking pretty, "abriendo en corazón sus boquitas de pez hambriento, en equilibrio" (13). Before a large window, they double up like mirror images:

> Ya están las dos sentadas, compuestas, ante un ventanal de celuloide. Ni una mancha, ni un solo cabello desplazado, ni una gota de salsa de tomate en las mejillas. Fijas; las cabezas, separadas unos centímetros, coinciden con el cruce de las diagonales del paisaje, (16).

Centered in a "landscape" taken from a sketching primer, they share the distress of having found the "Domus Dei" empty. Even momentarily "fixed," still, they have to appear by what they lack: "ni una mancha, ni un solo cabello..." They are doubles, doubled by a celluloid window, a screen/mirror in which pespective is a flat hoax; psychological depth, a forgotten fantasy.

After the visit to the empty "Domus Dei," Auxilio overcomes her distress by passing out photographs among the diners at the self-sevice: "A cada entrega sonríe, se da un peinazo, se presenta al destinatario con una reverencia y renueva su asombro con la descripción minuciosa de la foto" (17). The photographs, another flat surface which mimics depth, depict subsequent incarnations of the pair. In one Auxilio wears a "guayabera," one of the disguises used in the next section by the elusive Flor de Loto. In another, Auxilio wears the gown of a Ming empress, again

---

[5] *Antología de lingüística cubana* 2: 132.

alluding to the Chinese diva of *Junto al Río de Cenizas de Rosas*. The characters are all versions of Auxilio and Socorro, inseparable signifying unit whose presence in the text not only inverts the values of anthropomorphic characterization but subverts them into oblivion. Forster's categories of "round" and "flat" cannot contain them, whether "round" or "flat," the character described in *Aspects of the Novel* is the lieutenant of an absent, psychologically resonant entity. Sarduy's characters are agents of another sort, of a subjectivity whose only claim to resonance is the text.

The narrative moves from Auxilio-Socorro's doubling to their meeting with a third party, the General, one of the versions of Mortal. Breaking from Socorro, Auxilio tangles her wig in the General's medals and the two become a twoheaded creature: "serpientes emplumadas – cheek to cheek," glued to each other, Siamese twins, "Murciélago de la Bacardí," inkblot... (19) The pair "absorbs" everything around it, including the two characters which appear in the subsequent narratives, the Chinese diva and Dolores Rondón: "así el binomio Auxilio-General chupó todo lo que había alrededor, y claro está, chupó a una negra y a una china: así se completó el curriculum cubense" (20). The "cube" includes the characters of the Chinese diva, "una asiática empolvada con cascarilla," Dolores, "una negra de redondas nalgas y pechos," and a fourth element, Death, "la Pelona Innombrable," attached to the General, the emblem of power. Dolores and the Chinese diva are versions of Auxilio and Socorro, who now appear in the cube as the supplements of characterization.

Taking it from the top, reflected in a mirror that hangs from above the cash register, the figure of the four characters looks like a four-leaf clover: "el conjunto es un trébol gigante de cuatro hojas, o un animal de cuatro cabezas que miran hacia los cuatro puntos cardinales, o un signo yoruba de los cuatro caminos" (20-21). There are four characters, the General, a Chinese diva, a black woman of Rubenesque proportions, and Death, "la Sola-Vaya." The number four is emphasized throughout this section. The "gato boca" which accompanies the Chinese diva represents the number four in the Cuban numbers' game or "charada." Enrico Mario Santí has identified the number four in the *Curriculum* with Heidegger's Fourfold (earth, heaven, man and gods), which suggests that the novel, given the relative explicitness of

Sarduy's reference to Heidegger, "is unable to escape the ontological question," in spite of the parody, the *choteo,* of such a question present in the narrative.[6] However, if the novel cannot escape the ontological question, it does attempt to sidestep two exclusive propositions: that is, that the novel is either a Heideggerian search for identity or a nihilistic "total fiction" which rejects the possibility of such a search. Sarduy's plural text wants it both ways. The final note of the novel seems to break the unity of the "four" composed by the other sections, subverting the authority of Heideggerian metaphysics, as well as the no less transcendent notion of textual autonomy.

Heidegger's "way to language," is centered on the notion of "Saying," which "will not let itself be captured in any statement." It conceals not only the being of language but the secret of man's origin. The poet is the name-giver, whose "nondenial of self" corresponds "to the mystery of the word," the word as *logos.*[7] Santí suggests that there may be more than a trace of *choteo* in all of this; it does seem unlikely, in spite of the reference to Heidegger, that Sarduy, trickster and doubletalker, would throw in the ontological towel this early in the game. Whether the final note is "part of the fiction" or "an authorial directive" almost begs the question. Perhaps it is both, and it is neither. If to put pen to paper is already an ontological move, then any writing, no matter how materialistic its intent, would undertake a metaphysical replay. *De donde son los cantantes* may not break the confines of such a replay, but the text does attempt a radical recasting. What the text privileges is the gesture of the hand in writing, endlessly repeated, and perhaps more mysterious than the veils of ontology. In González Echevarría's reading of *De donde,* the four parts become a "cosmograma congo" which questions the authority of the Heideggerian fourfold.[8] The dialogic quality of the novel not only tolerates both designs but encourages their confrontation and overlapping. Such a pattern of inclusion/rejection is characteristic of the novel. As suggested by Santí and

---

[6] Enrico Mario Santí, "Textual Politics: Severo Sarduy," *Latin American Literary Review* 8.16 (1980): 158.

[7] Martin Heidegger, *On the Way to Language,* trans. Peter D. Hertz (New York: 1971) 134-151.

[8] *La ruta de Severo Sarduy* 123.

González Echevarría, the novel provokes a particular reading, while sowing at the same time the seeds of its undoing.

What takes precedence in the text is the double presence of Auxilio and Socorro, textual vehicles of an absent subject and harbingers of death, "la Gran Pelona." Just as the absent subject depends on the semiotic pair to carry on the narrative, Death presents the other side of the signifying process; it is the non-marked, the non-signifying. The General appears as one of the versions of Mortal, a reader-figure associated with the pursuit of a "message" that the text refuses to yield. In the final section of the novel, Mortal-Christ becomes the one pursued and at the same time a textual figure for the absent subject. Yet the emphasis remains on Auxilio-Socorro. Their role in Sarduy's fiction is triadic; yet their doubling suggests another fourfold, the doubling of the "simulacrum," where no veils are parted, where no signifier, privileged or otherwise, has the final say, the realm of an affirmation, the coming of a "world of signs," where guilt, truth, and origin are superseded by an "active interpretation," off-center, a celebration of the excentric.[9]

From the pair Auxilio/General two other characters emanate, the Chinese diva and Dolores, who later appears as protagonist of one of the narratives. In the *Curriculum Cubense,* the figure that "shines in its absence" is as much an allusion to an improbable metaphysics as it is a reference to the absent subject who produces the text and whose role is not limited to that of an implicit author but who is present in every aspect of the narrative. The "author" is yet another figure in the narrative whose claim to power is constantly questioned by the actions of the pair Auxilio-Socorro.

When Socorro first addresses Auxilio, the author comments, "es Socorro la que habla," in an aside to the reader. Thus the author as a role in the text alternates with the discourse of the other characters in which an absent subject signals his presence through an allusive process directed at a potential reader, who may tune in to references to Max Factor and Quevedo, or tune out to references to Vasarély. The presence of the reader is

---

[9] J. Derrida, *L'écriture et la différence* (Paris: Seuil, 1967) 427. See also Richard Klein, "Prolegomenon to Derrida," *Diacritics* 2.4 (1972): 29-34.

constantly demanded, and his flight is a possibility recognized in the text. When Auxilio and Socorro give out photographs at the self-service, mimicking the delivery of the text itself, Socorro warns, "Pero vámonos antes de que se arrepientan" (18).

The subjective absence associated with author and reader is further signalled by the third person pronoun that appears from the beginning of the *Curriculum Cubense*. In an attempt to recover her composure, Socorro suggests, "Cantemos: siempre ausente, siempre ausente/ hace el mal gratuitamente" (12). Auxilio sings along, adding, " – Sí, es él. La adivinanza de las adivinanzas. La pregunta de los sesenta y cuatro mil dólares, la definición del ser." If the Benvenistian third person pronoun never reflects the instance of discourse, it serves to allude to that which may be absent from the process of narration. The "él" who does harm becomes a figure of absence which dramatizes the role of a writing subject only intermittently identified as an authorial figure. Like the God that Socorro fails to find in the "Domus Dei," the subject also "Brilla por su ausencia" (13). The state of metaphysical hunger which propels Auxilio and Socorro in their search for God is correlative to an ontological reading which the text tries to subvert. The traces in writing of a definition of being, "la definición del ser," are refracted at every turn.

When the metaphysically searching author tries to intrude in the text more boldly, Auxilio and Socorro shout, "Lo único que faltaba: ¡el escritor Dios, el que lo ve todo y mete la nariz en todas partes menos donde debe!" (31). They mock the teller of the tale as a would-be omniscient author, who turns out to be on the same level with the other characters. The mocking of the omniscient author further distances this type of narrative voice from the biographical alibi of the signer of the text. The writing subject is not allowed to "incarnate" as an authorial figure, even an implicit one; he is as much a part of the characters, ("desde él" flows Auxilio's hair), as he is "lo único que faltaba," the intruding author silenced by the pair, put in his place. The characters carry on a dialog which reveals the limitations of a characterization based on naming, action, description, narrative voices, pronouns, implicit authors, in short, the stock in trade of fiction. What is suggested instead is that the text shuffles the fragments of a writer's persona, that in one of those fragments a reader may recognize a fragment of his own, and keep on reading.

In a final section of the *Curriculum Cubense* titled "Una nueva versión de los hechos: Parca y General," the author, already stripped of authority, tells of the encounter between Auxilio and the General in a direct tone which mocks the conventions of authorial impartiality. The author pretends to take down all that he "sees," addressing the reader in a rhetorical first person plural: "Anotemos pues, tal y como se ve en estos instantes: frente al departamento de postres..." (19). By this point, his intentions to jot down exactly what is "seen" have an effect similar to the hyperbolic insults and the constant metamorphoses of Auxilio and Socorro, part of the process which undermines the referent, particularly Sarduy the signer as referent. At the end of this section, an authorial figure takes on the first person pronoun, proffering three adjectives which are immediately dismissed by Auxilio as one of the excesses of the new literature: "En mi tiempo no era así. A dónde va la joven literatura..." (20). "En mi tiempo" is a literary past, and "A dónde" is its future, but neither the "yo" nor Auxilio have the authority to define such limits. The "past" of literature, Auxilio's "En mi tiempo," and its future, the "A dónde va" of an exhausted avant-garde, belong to a system whose idealistic linearity *De donde son los cantantes* tries to sidestep at every turn, in order to ask the reader to suspend his beliefs in those categories, to focus on the text with the right kind of concentration.

Subsequently, the "yo" fades in and out; thrashed by Auxilio-Socorro, it never comes close to approaching the outerlimits of authority, signalling instead its role as "shifter," as empty sign. Far from alluding to a human plenitude, it signals the linguistic dependence of such plenitude, and drains it of the metaphor of vitality, leaving the pronoun as a shell, now literally floating, adrift, only temporarily filled by the reader.

The pattern set for characterization in the opening section is carried out throughout the other narratives in *De donde son los cantantes*. If the subject is the absent one, "siempre ausente, siempre ausente/ hace el mal gratuitamente" (12), this absence and its correlative desire structure the narratives that make up the novel. The General desires Flor de Loto, a false vision concocted by Auxilio-Socorro. Dolores Rondón desires fame and power, and Auxilio and Socorro throw themselves into the search for Mortal. At the same time, the quest of the characters duplicates the desire of the fragmented subject, divided in the language in which he has cast his lot, having had the biographical rug pulled out from under him, banished from the depths of meaning, invested in an array of words, the place of his fragmentary constitution.

In *Junto al Río,* the General searches for the object he desires, the images of Flor, singer in the Chinese theater. The theater is the setting for the appearances of Flor, and the General tries to gain access to the space of his desire. His efforts double those of a reader who may try to penetrate "the meaning" of the text – the rhetoric of reading is full of breaking and entering imagery. When "El Lector" complains about the incongruity of a Marlene Dietrich record in the "Chinese" setting, he is put in his place by "Yo." Alongside the recurring first person, the authorial role in this section is also invested in a character called "El Director," a reefer smoking choreographer. Standing in the empty proscenium, "El Director" feels the gaze of two eyes, "ojillos de neón verde, paralelos," set in the cracks on the stage floor. The references to cracks, stripes, or fissures, Auxilio as a striped bird, Vasarély's zebras, recur, as if to allude to the textual interstices where the subject lodges. "Afuera," outside the theatre, metaphorically the realm of the real, where a naturalistc "tísico del cine cambia la cartelera," the striped visage also lurks, "una cara con franjas negras y amarillas como un pez indio" (29).

The Director becomes a figure for the author as the manipulator of his characters. He is a puppetter, who along with an assistant, controls the movements of Auxilio and Socorro. The characters replay the spastic movements of the Western puppet, "animated" by a hidden force in a comical version of dualistic metaphysics, body/soul, man/God, characters/author. The General's effort to enter the theater break the spell; the Director lets go of the strings, and Auxilio and Socorro, "las Culito," literally fall on their ass, and with them goes the role of the Director-Author as puller of strings, tier of narrative knots.

The General desires Flor, also called La Ming, "una ausencia pura," the object of a love quest and also the locale of the prized reward for the kind of dualism associated with the Director-Puppetmaster's handling of Auxilio-Socorro; Flow would be "the soul" behind "las Obesas," Auxilio-Socorro's all too solid textual flesh, the "opacity" of their symbolic presence. However, all the General gets is substitution, supplement, disguise; he can have the pair as leather boys, but not Flor: "Acaba de consumar con las Dos – y juntas – , la impostura que suponéis" (38). He turns into "el Mirón," if not getting what he wants, perhaps finding what he needs by masturbating while watching María Eng, one more version of the original pair, and Johnny, an American sailor, as they make love: "estaba en su nirvana el mirón, y de la pura contemplación, ya había pasado a la praxis da solo. Se olvidaba de Flor. ¿La superponía (y él al míster) en aquel dúo?" (44). The mirrored images become for him an obsession with an absence that cannot be satisfied: "La Ausencia le come el hígado – cirrosis ontológica – ." The General's erotico-ontological desire is not satisfied, turning his efforts to enter the theatre into a metaphysical quest: "el teatro se volvió para G. una misa" (49).

The General's frustration in the end turns love into cruelty, and he gives up, opening a nearby store called "*La Divina Providencia,* tienda total," which supplies the theatre (54). The proliferation of signifiers, associated with the comings and goings of Auxilio and Socorro, is all that remains. Flor vanishes, and the General's frustration becomes correlative with that of a reader who may have expected a "message" from the text, something to relieve his own ontological longings. The objections of such a reader are either set aside, silenced or ignored. After an argument between the General and "yo" over the facts, the reader as the character of "El Lector," interrupts:

> –Bueno, pónganse de acuerdo: una versión o la otra. Lo que yo quiero son hechos. Sí, hechos, acción, desarrollo, mensaje, en suma. ¡Mensaje lírico! (49)

The reader's demand is not met and the narrative ends melodramatically, with the General awaiting the death of Flor, when in fact what follows is the resurgence of Auxilio-Socorro, the immortal ones.

In his search for the object of his desire, the General craves the one who would satisfy an erotico-ontological need, that would heal the absence that constitutes him and that drives him to the feast of ever-deceiving signifiers. His desired object, his "petit-a," is embodied by Auxilio-Socorro in the theater where Flor is said to appear. His wants correspond to the desire for the settling of a subjective pact: "Quiere el doble, el simétrico, el ludión que pasa del otro lado de la escena para darse a sí mismo la réplica – tú y yo – , que se vira como un guante, (39). But the subjectivity inscribed in the text is not a given bound by pronominal certainties, "tú y yo." If the General cannot cap his search with a satisfactory final term, object or signified, neither can writer nor reader rest assured in an intersubjectivity merely dependent on the shared properties of two personal pronouns, however "empty" they might be. The dialogue of subjects is oblique, elusive, a peculiar effect of language, dialogic, but not necessarily a dialogue.

The final narrative in *De donde son los cantantes, La Entrada de Cristo en La Habana,* uses the same characters that appear in *Junto al Río,* but their roles are reversed. In *Junto al Río,* Auxilio and Socorro mask the ontological presence of a desired object, cruelly teasing the General in his state of longing; on the other hand, in *La Entrada de Cristo,* the pair seeks the desired term, now dramatized by Mortal-Christ, a figure which is again the focus of erotic, ontological desire. In the last tale of the novel, the decomposition of the desired term, and the affirmation of the signifying pair constitute the adventure of a deconstruction of the Saussurean sign. The destruction of the third term, Mortal-Christ, undermines a triadic scheme and at the same time unravels the Christian trinity that depends on it. In the same way that the role of the reader is projected into the vain search of the General in the first narrative, the decomposing body of Mortal-Christ in the last one becomes the final emblem of the deferral of the subject.

In *La Entrada de Cristo* the writing subject signals his veiled presence through the same devices adumbrated in the *Curriculum Cubense.* His style involves a constant rewriting of other texts, from the early chronicles of the conquest to the icons of early pop culture. If in the *Curriculum,* a recurring "Yo" is put in its place, *La Entrada* is the story of "El," the absent God, and of the writer/reader as the absences that obliquely inform the narrative. The decomposing figure of Mortal-Christ alludes to the dispersion of the text, to its shattering of the subject. Mortal-Christ is the "Face-Giver": "Soy el que da Rostro. El que más dice. Mía es ya la hoja del Códice. Mía la tinta y lo pintado" (143). The sky, a crumpled paper, "papel estrujado," marked by tracings, "ondas lentas: resaca de una salina" refers to the text as the place where the markings of "el que da Rostro" are etched. The end of the narrative is presented as the decomposition of Mortal-Christ and of the subject who has depended on the text to acquiere a provisional visage.

The relationship between the subject as absence and the text as the provisional composition of a persona, which plays out as the narrative ends, corresponds in the last section of the novel to the decay of Mortal-Christ and the activities of the signifying pair, Auxilio-Socorro. As Mortal decomposes in his Westbound journey through the territory of Cuban culture, Auxilio and Socorro seek his redemption by making of their bodies a text with Mortal's name inscribed on it. Auxilio buys a printing kit, and exclaims, "Haré de mi cuerpo Tu libro,/ ileerán de mí!" (137). She covers her body with the letters of Mortal's name: "se estampó la primera letra en una nalga ... desde el ombligo, que irradiaba una O, hasta el punto y aparte de la rodilla le fulgían las letras" (137). Auxilio/Socorro/text spell out the name of Mortal while his body vanishes; they spell out a name, the subject's biography, cast into the erotic commerce of language.

In *Junto al Río* and *La Entrada de Cristo,* the signifiers' plurality affirms the illusory unity of the subject, transforming anthropomorphic alibi into the legible visage of a textual hero. The subject is in the characters, in the pronouns, ever figured, never manifest. Yet this subject-hero is haunted by the double of the man, the distant signer, Severo, who appears in the advertising periphery of *De donde son los cantantes,* in a photograph: from Camagüey, like Dolores; born in 1937; author of *Gestos,* etc. The photograph affirms an illusory, phantasmagoric corporeal unity, the Lacanian "mirage" of the body's wholeness. Back at the self-service of the *Curriculum,* Auxilio had pulled out fifty color photos, discarded two and handed Socorro a black-and-white close-up. The discarded image, an i.d. picture "en la cual se ve de frente ... tal cual es," may be Severo's own, included on the back of the book, not allowed in the main body of the text. The photograph's glorification of unity is off-limits; the subject's place is another, ineluctably shattered, constituted in the traffic of the letter.

The signer's biography is replayed in the section titled *La Dolores Rondón,* a story supposedly based on the life of a real woman from Camagüey.[10] It tells of the rise and fall of a provincial "mulata," succintly recorded in her one literary effort, her epitaph, engraved on her gravestone. The narrative, the dramatized commentary of the epitaph's verses, plays on the familiar topos of the relationship between the poet's life and his work. The story is opened by an authorial guide who invites the reader to stroll through the graveyard in Camagüey where Dolores is buried. This mock authorial voice, a replay of the *Curriculum*'s "Yo", casually refers to Camagüey, birthplace of poets, and affirms the myth of the redeeming power of art, "Pero el poeta nos mira, desde la muerte" (57), a melodramatic aside which sets the tone for the theatrical conceit which structures the narrative.

The "reality" of Dolores, based on the suggestion that Dolores "existió realmente," contrasts with another one of her "sources." *Dolores* is the title of a novella by Camagüey's Gertrudis Gómez de Avellaneda, based on a character who also "existió realmente," the author tells us in an introductory letter.[11] The story of Avellaneda's Dolores, set in the fifteenth century, bears no resemblance to Sarduy's; however, the tone of the narrator who opens each story does. The confident, familiar deictics of Sarduy's narrator, "Aquí, por ejemplo," his editorial "dejemos" to the reader, matches the Avellaneda narrator's attitude toward the reader: "El lector comprenderá, por tanto, sin necesidad de mayores explicaciones" (97). The latter's narrative ends with the following epitaph, "Aquí yace María de las Dolores Gómez de Sandoval y Avellaneda" (120). Sarduy's of course begins and ends with the epitaph, "Aquí Dolores Rondón." In La Avellaneda's romantic tale, the eponymous protagonist supposedly dies in her youth, only to turn up years later as a pious nun. At the end, the ornate tomb intended for the young Dolores remains empty, while the "other" Dolores is buried in a grave marked only by a cross.

---

[10] Concepción T. Alzola, "*Verba Cubanorum:* El habla popular en *De Dónde Son los Cantantes,*" [sic] *Cinco aproximaciones a la narrativa hispanoamericana contemporánea,* ed. Gladys Zaldívar (Madrid: Nova Scholar, 1977) 19-20. Alzola, who also draws a parallel between the life of Cuban vedette Rita Montaner and Dolores Rondón's *décima,* affirms that Dolores "existió realmente."

[11] *Biblioteca de Autores Españoles* (Madrid: Atlas, 1981) vol. 5. Subsequent references in the text by page number in parenthesis.

The parallel with Sarduy's Dolores, influenced as she is by "los clásicos cubanos," is significant. Sarduy's Dolores is centered, on her poem, on her name, on her ornate grave, in Camagüey, "en el centro de Cuba" (57), on the corporeity of her double, buried somewhere in Camagüey. Yet she has a literary double in la Avellaneda's Dolores, supposedly the poet's ancestor who also "existió realmente," but who is transparently built on a romantic conceit, her name inscribed on a fancy grave, "la tumba vacía," her body lying in an humble place marked only by a cross. La Avellaneda's Dolores ends up with two graves, an empty one with her bombastic name cut into the slab, the place where she is mourned; the other one marked only by a cross, nameless, her body forgotten.

The story of Sarduy's Dolores also begins with a ridiculously ornate grave, "Bajo el poema dos ángeles boca abajo sostienen una lámpara encendida" (57), a fit beginning for her programmed rise and fall. Through the character of Dolores, Sarduy jives at various literary traditions, defunct or waning, particularly a quaint brand of folkloric spontaneity, which pretends, for the sake of an always naive, willing reader, that a popular lore is the casual, yet vital, substratum of a popular literature, masking all the while the tricks of the writer's trade either behind an accepted tradition or behind the facade of autobiography or family anecdote—"una crónica de familia" is the subtitle of la Avellaneda's *Dolores*. Of course, the writer knows all along that not all readers buy "the legend" wholesale, that some may see the mastery of the craftsman's hand behind the scenes. Max Henríquez Ureña doubts the verisimilitude imposed on the novel by Avellaneda herself, and writes, "La fantasía de la autora ha debido intervenir."[12] Even in Avellaneda's fanciful legends, one may find traces of the poet's "self-portrait."[13]

With Sarduy there is no "behind the scenes." The boundary imposed by the proscenium arch, the setting for the histrionics of

---

[12] *Panorama histórico de la literatura cubana*, 2 vols. (Puerto Rico: Mirador, 1963) 1: 223-224.
[13] María A. Salgado, "El arte de la leyenda en Gertrudis Gómez de Avellaneda," *Homenaje a Gertrudis Gómez de Avellaneda* (Miami: Universal, 1981) 338-346.

Dolores, which insures a type of representational illusion, crumbles, just as the threads holding the puppets break in *Junto al Río*. Dolores Rondón and Dolores Gómez are both paper creatures, masking their textuality behind the propriety/property of their proper name, joyfully pointing to a "living" referent. The quotation marks around "living" are annoying, yet necessary, not because all referentiality requires such bracketing, but because in the case of the two Dolores, both names point to a grave, grandly kitsch, and empty, the mausoleum of literature, ransacked, pillaged, and plundered in *De donde son los cantantes*.

Dolores's story is initially "told" by the two "Narradores" whose professorial comments on the value of literature contrast throughout with the protagonist's vital élan. The detached posture of the authorial figure who introduces "La Dolores Rondón" as he turns the story over to the narrators, ("dejemos la palabra a los dos narradores"), suggests that the story is told following the very conventions which are undermined in the two narratives framing this section. However, the limitations of the narrators' role are immediately evident, and the two are joined by Auxilio-Socorro, the ever-present ones without whom the show cannot go on, supplemented by a third, Clemencia, transforming the double into a triangle, emblem of the trinitarian nostalgia characteristic of *La Dolores Rondón*.

The discussion of the Narradores about the value of literature parodies the rhetoric of existential dialectics, ("con palabras se modifican las cosas, los comportamientos"), which alludes to one of the passwords of the "committed" writer, lifted from Sartre: "L'écrivain 'engagé' sait que la parole est action." The phrase is from *Qu'est-ce que la littérature?*, the handbook of the committed writer, which was, incidentally, dedicated to "Dolorès," another fitting ancestor of Sarduy's existential, earthy Dolores and her Nothing Shakes.[14] The character of Dolores, based after all on a real life person, is given a body whose fullness seems to attest to its referential claim on life: "una negra de redondas nalgas y pechos, muy semicircular, muy cosena" (20). Yet her hair, "un río de lianas," and her eventual baldness bind her to Auxilio-Socorro, from whom she issued to begin to with in the *Curricu-*

---

[14] (Paris: Gallimard, 1948) 9-44.

lum Cubense. Dolores is not Forster's psychologically "round" character; she is literally round, but she is also in her grave from the start, and Auxilio and Socorro, pretending to be her servants, have the last word. The death of Dolores is the death of the referential double, and the transformation of death into something other than a metaphysically charged final chapter.

The failure of Dolores as a dancer at the presidential palace is followed by Mortal's political downfall; he is accused of dealing in prostitution, among other things, "trata de blancas" (79). The phrase alludes to the title of a naturalistic novel, *Trata de blancas,* written by Eugenio Antonio Flores and reviewed by Julián del Casal, who called it "la historia repugnante, descarada y vulgar de las mujeres pobres," poor women who came to Cuba to become prostitutes, direct ancestors of the peripatetic Dolores.[15] Dolores has been affected by her reading of "los clásicos cubanos" (76), and her story is Sarduy's paean to his literary roots. Her full body itself is a figure of Guillenesque proportions; her voluptuous rear seems particularly indebted to that of María Belén Chacón, endowed with "los espejos redondos y alegres de tus dos nalgas," the subject of Emilio Ballagas's "Elegía."[16] Supposedly based on a real woman, the character of Dolores is nevertheless a moving quotation. Her character "cites" the popular heroine, the colorful "mulata," the existential heroine, the living legend, even the tragic heroine whose dying speech she parrots: "Puñal, sé breve" (63), not to mention Rita Montaner.

In her move toward fame and fortune, the character of Dolores parodies the view of literature as the saving antidote to life's sordid demands. Her will to become someone else, to redefine her identity parodies the quest of the existential hero whose vital defeat insures a different kind of victory, moral, metaphysical. Ludicrously, what Unamuno writes of Dante may also be said of Dolores, "Política, religión y poesía fueron en él y para él una sola cosa, una íntima trinidad;"[17] but in *De donde son los cantantes,* this is said of Dolores in a second, or third degree,

---

[15] *Prosas* 2: 84.

[16] Emilio Ballagas, *Obra poética* (Miami: Mnemosyne Publishing Inc., 1969) 66-67.

[17] *Cómo se hace una novela* 164. Subsequent references in the text by page number in parenthesis.

whose spirals trap the reader and make him accomplice in a subjectivity which, as it works itself out, unravels the severe contrasts which structure the "living legend" of Dolores. The character of Dolores parodies Unamuno's conception of man as "autor de ti mismo," and man as a "criatura de ficción," man as the master of his destiny, whether through words or through actions. In *Cómo se hace una novela,* Unamuno restates his view of fiction as autobiography, because if a work of fiction "lives," it is because, for him, it is in a sense autobiographical: "los autores, los poetas, nos ponemos, nos creamos en todos los personajes poéticos que creamos" (129). No such "creation" is at work in *De donde son los cantantes.*

The character of Dolores oversteps the limits of such a creation, and the vitalistic myth that lurks behind it. On the level of the story, her own ambition is her undoing. She's predetermined by her origins, "el lugar de su origen" (60), which she disdains to become something else, to master her destiny, like a character from Unamuno, whose self-determination should signal to the reader the possibility of his own independence. In a world ruled by the moralistic Narrators, Dolores pays dearly for her centered self. But her payment is cancelled; her check bounces. Not only are the Narradores ludicrous from the start, the death of Dolores, her payment for a misguided life, corresponds to a naturalistic characterization which is turned upside down, turned inside out. Such a characterization goes hand in hand with the truth of fiction, and with the correlative veracity of history. But for Dolores, it was Columbus who burned the ships, the Condesa de Merlín is really from Berlín, and her reading of Cuban literary history has driven her mad– "Las lecturas le han hecho mucho daño. La han enloquecido (76). The order of things in the world in which she shines for a moment is inverted, so that the meaning of her push to arrive at her "destiny" ("llegaré a mi destino puntualmente, como un tren americano") in the context defined by her and the Narradores is altered through a ludicrous characterization.

A realistic characterization, whether founded on a living model or on Unamuno's existential pact with the reader, corresponds to the meaning Dolores seeks, but her will to move remains confined to the novel; her *"bovarysme"* is precisely *"insatisfaction romanesque," "pouvoir qu'a l'homme de se concevoir autre qu'il n'est"* says Robert's dictionary. Dolores's characterization hinges on that second, useless negative. She comes on as a character, wanting to grow, to have a destiny, and ends up as an expletive, a pleonastic shifter in the long phrase that is her story, a photographic negative of the realistic, regional Cuban novel – "ni los aguaceros, ni los charcos, ni las carretas con bueyes, ni las campañas electorales" (60).

With the Narradores and their hairsplitting arguments on the value of literature put aside, framed by their own proscenium arch theatricality, the resurgence of the Ever-present Ones, Auxilio-Socorro, is ineluctable, protest though one might– "¡Ah no, eso sí que no! A esas tres locas no las soporto" (59). Their duplicity, which insured the doubling of the *Curriculum Cubense* is transformed in this section into a trinity completed by Clemencia, Mercy for the transcendental longings of Dolores. But it's a provisional mercy, so that the story can be told– "para que el poema se vaya cumpliendo paso a paso (cosa que ya comienza a aburrirnos) y sin tropiezos" (68). But the text ruled by Auxilio-Socorro, is made up precisely of "tropiezos," stabs in the dark, crabwalks, and the pair becomes bored with the linearity associated with Dolores and Mortal, also a citer of worn-out discourses whose "destiny" would blend with that of "his people," but whose initial "yo" is cut off by the commercials on the radio, signifiers with a single distant message – "buy"; and by static, signifiers with no message; so that Mortal's "mensaje" empties of meaning as it is uttered.

When Mortal uses the word "entusiasmado," Narrador Uno mocks him for not knowing its root: *éntheos,* having god within. Mortal persists, foreshadowing his own death as a god in the last section. The gods, and with them transcendence, trinity, and meaning as the ready effect of the signifier, flee in the first section of the novel; yet through Mortal's faith, ridiculed by the ludicrous Narradores, the text points not to the ironic rescuing of meaning, but to the oblique signalling of its passing. In this way, the text subverts its own insistent *choteo.* "Que el relajo sea con orden," says "El peluquero" (Socorro). In the *choteo'*s jive at authority, directed from below, there is an implicit recognition of impotence, and an ultimate return to the order of things, only fleetingly upset by the mocker's quick lash.[18] Sarduy's text suggests a more serious blow, a stab toward a new order of things, not merely the immanent order of the text as closed artifact, but an ongoing epistemological recasting in which his work, however modestly, aims to figure.

The Narradores manipulate an aspect of the mechanics of textuality, the craft of fiction, and an authorial figure at the beginning of *La Dolores* steps aside in a Flaubertian gesture of distancing, opening the possibility that the tale is a parody of the realistic novel, whose paragon would be *Madade Bovary*, the story of another bored country girl with a penchant for pretty things. But a parody respects its model; it recharges it with a different kind of value. That being the case, the tale of *La Dolores*, the physical center of *De donde son los cantantes*, would restate Percy Lubbock's classic question, "But which *is* the centre, which is the mind that really commands the subject?".[19] Yet what *Dolores* questions is not so much the supposedly seamless fiction in Flaubert's novel as a reading of the novel based on what Forster called Lubbock's "'aesthetics of fiction,'" on the truth of fiction affirmed by the master formalists. Such a reading of fiction depends on contradictory affirmations: the fictional status of the character on the one hand, and its possession of an "inner life" on the other, a duality which replays the attendant opposites, outside/inside, objectivity/subjectivity, truth/fiction, body/soul, signifier/signified. While praising Lubbock for his rigor, Forster prefers a reading that would be more of a "'ramshackly survey.'"[20]

For Lubbock, Madame Bovary's limitations as a "subject" are supplemented by "the author's wit" – "none other, must supply what is wanting" (87). A clue to Flaubert's genius lies in his ability to reveal that "wit" without ever cracking the veneer that holds Emma together, without showing that "Her pair of eyes is not enough" (86). By contrast, Sarduy's novel is full of cracks and peering eyes, and the fact that its "subject" is not contained in

---

[18] For a discussion of Jorge Mañac's *choteo, Indagación del choteo* (1940; rpt. Miami, Fla.: Mnemosyne, 1969), see Gustavo Pérez Firmat, *Literature and Liminality* 51-108.

[19] *The Craft of Fiction* (1921; New York: Viking Compass Edition, 1957) 74.

[20] Quoted by Mark Schorer, "Foreword to the Compass Edition" *The Craft of Fiction*, n.p. Subsequent references in the text by page number in parenthesis.

any one character or point of view constantly affirms not only a Bakhtinian plurality, but a fundamental "alienation" which, on the level of narrative, structures the tale, not the alienation of the historical subject, but that of the divided subject, insisting/existing on the one hand as a by-product of the signifying process, exiting on the other, condemned to a "fading" even as it appears.

In the case of Dolores, the photographic metaphor of characterization used in *Curriculum* resurfaces– she's the negative of the realistic heroine whose limitations as a subject are overcome by the broader "point of view" of the fiction in which her "life" is inscribed– "mi vida escrita en una piedra" (83). As for the subject of *De donde son los cantantes,* his "picture," "tamaño seis por ocho," his image "tal cual es," having strutted its brief hour, is condemned to fading, to the obscurely semiotic, pre-fictional lacunas of non-sense; he is eclipsed in what Auxilio calls "la cualidad espiral del tiempo del ser" (68), not an ontological quality, but a subjective one.

As the death of Dolores approaches, Auxilio and Socorro save the day by ignoring her plight and its moral dimensions within the confines of the narrative, and transforming her name to "Do-la-res," so that the show can go on; for dollar/money/sign guarantees the symbolic exchanges on which the displacement of the text depends. Auxilio and Socorro, Dolores's guardian angels, serve her as best they can. Remember that Dolores is duped in her reading of the Cuban classics; among other things, she thinks Columbus, not Cortés, burned the ships, and that "Merlín" is "Berlín." Auxilio and Socorro latch on to these errors, and make of her end, not the dreaded arrival of "la Pelona," the Baldie Reaper, but a conditional stopping place punctuated by the final, Nietzschean "¡Sí!" If "Do-lo-res" can change into "Do-la-res," the death of Dolores may not be the end of *Dolores;* one is transformed into the other through the good offices of Auxilio-Socorro. If one letter may be substituted for another, the chain may continue, an opportunity seized by the metonymic pair, hungry for a code, even a dress code, "De Schiaparelli, Chanel y Christian Dior." Dolores's last "pesos," destined for "la luz y el agua," metaphysically loaded signifiers, are traded in, as Dolores makes her grand exit, for another unessential, yet necessary, multiplying chain, *"Duke al piano, Cootie Williams a la trompeta, Ray Nance al violín, Chuck Connors al trombón-bajo, etc.*

(87). "Así se pierde lo esencial" (86), but with none of the silly solemnity of the Narradores. The end is a jazzy jig. The fading of the subject is neither solemn, nor nihilistic; it is inseparable from desire, the proper province of the subject, a "character" insinuated beyond characterization, or story, or theme. The provisional end of his trajectory is also perhaps the beginning of a possible bracketing of desire. When all is (nearly) said and done, the necessary tricks of the writer's trade, story, plot, characterization, are all for naught, if they do not open the way to the shared specificity of a traced experience.

III
Writing: the affective mark

1: THE PLAY'S THE THING

Among the Nambikwara of Brazil the meeting between different tribes follows a peculiar pattern. A warrior grabs his penis and points it at a member of the other tribe to indicate aggression, a gesture accompanied by the tense exchange of phrases which alternate insult and reconciliation. There follows an equally tense mutual inspection of each other's goods and ornaments, which each inspector demands of the other. The ritual is a prelude to the actual exchange of goods, a commerce in various merchandises which can last half a day. Over time, the initial gestures of violence build up resentment and may lead to war, to real violence, suspended as long as the exchange of goods is carried on.[1] In this tribe, the pointing of the penis in a gesture of agression gives way to an oblatory stage in which violence is deferred and goods are exchanged. The shopping habits of the Nambikwara are far from the realm of *De donde son los cantantes,* but the pattern of violence/exchange may suggest another approach to it.

Sarduy's novel may be the place where the elided subject shows his falling feathers, "el pájaro pintor de Lacan," a prelude to the third-degree "autobiographical" flights of *Colibrí.* Few texts are as obsessively allusive as *De donde son los cantantes;* Freud, Lacan, Derrida, Max Factor, even Lukács, have their cameos. Yet the text resists a Lacanian or a Freudian, a Derridian, or a Lukácsian reading for that matter. The allusions are there, but the significant patterns are in the novel itself, not in the

---

[1] C. Lévi-Strauss, *Tristes tropiques* (Paris: Plon, 1955) 346-349.

hallowed enclosure of its pages, but in the reading you, or I, make of those patterns. The novel provides its own models for reading, for few texts reject hermetism as insistently as Sarduy's, whose obscurest citation is never far from a call to a potential reader, a desired, if fallible, interpreter. The pattern of violence/exchange of the Nambikwara may serve to reintroduce two final aspects to be discussed in this reading of *De donde:* the theatre and the question of the name.

In the *Curriculum Cubense,* Auxilio and Socorro exchange insults, but turn reverential toward the "destinatario" when handing out the photographs at the Self-Service. Their moves introduce an ambiguous relationship with the reader: the "lector baboso," the one who wants "mensaje" out of the text, and a confidential other obliquely addressed: "–Acérquense –les dijo–, mírenme bien" (143). In *Junto al Río,* the General, identified with the meaning-searching reader, enters a space where a man paints and where sailor Johnny shows "su sexo, rosado y perfectamente cilíndrico" (43), which reappers in *Maitreya,* "un miembro perfectamente cilíndrico."[2] In both novels, the phallus is set among a series of objects; in *De donde* it is transformed into a design on Johnny's shirt, "y en el amapola fluorescente de la camisa, como un caramelo o un reguilete."

There are no phallic symbols in Sarduy, nothing behind the phallus except the prelude to a series of terms. The phallus is not metaphoric in the narrow sense of popular psychology; its appearance always dramatizes a process of metonymy, of exchange and continuity. That is why in his search, the General is duped, and ends up waiting for a cadaverous meaning, Flor's corpse. The General's fate is a lesson to the common reader. The mausoleum of literature is full of meaning, ready for delivery. The reading of the text crosses over meaning with patterns of significance which must be pieced together: reading the pieces after the explosion in *Gestos,* or Auxilio and Socorro picking up bits of Mortal. At the end of *Junto al Río,* the phallus is an object among the many taken from *La Divina Providencia,* "tienda total," destined for Auxilio's "'salita pompeyana'" (52), already part of a cultural tradition in which the text and its readings are inscribed. Follow-

---

[2] (Barcelona: Barral, 1978) 108.

ing the allusive pattern of the novel, one may essay different "interpretations," to see where they may lead, and to abandon them as soon as the text, Sarduy's "jiribilla" slips the critic's procrustean hold.

Loaded down with the contents of the General's store, Auxilio insults the intruding authorial voice, as she shows him a huge decorative phallus "–Y tú, métete en lo que te importa, me cago en tu madre, para ti tengo esto" (52). The passage is rife with Freudian/Lacanian allusions. Auxilio aggressively points the phallus at an authorial figure, insults him, "shits" on his mother, as she piles even more things on her Vespa, which overflows and is supplemented by a pick-up truck. Freud's theories about childhood narcissism, the identification of the mother as phallic emblem, the mother as privileged receiver during the child's initial entrance into the symbolic order, the place of Lacan's Other, are implicit in this section. *Junto al Río* is a narcissistic, specular "stage" in the story. The General really wants his double, self satisfaction through the mirrored plenitude that is Flor. But such a move stops the metonymy of the text. He waits in vain. Auxilio and Socorro move on, and the final section of the novel *La Entrada de Cristo* is the place where the phallus is elliptically signalled: "señalándose con la otra el objeto de tan elípticos versos," referring to Bruno's singing "tengo una cosita que te gusta a ti" (128); also, "Se rascó lo que consideró más simbólico de la situación (¡ya tenía las manías cubanas!)" (133). After the splitting of the tapestry, the figure of the phallus is elided, and Auxilio and Socorro sustain the symbolic order, the pact with the reader they had initiated in the *Curriculum*. The General's punishment, having his nail pulled off, alludes to the Freudian metaphor of castration, which marks the individual's entrance into the symbolic order. In the final section, the place of the elided phallus, castration is assumed and transformed in the symbolic, supplementary activity of writing, as suggested in the elliptical reference to Bruno's "cosita." The text then moves to an oblatory realm, where an uneasy exchange is guaranteed, culminating in reconstituted Mortal's dancing exit into death. But Freud interprets dreams, and in *De donde son los cantantes* the only dreamer is the doomed Dolores. The novel may "flash" the unconscious, like the proverbial playground exhibitionist, but it ultimately skirts its ambiguous idealism.

I have followed the crude outlines of such a reading to suggest that it proves to be difficult to sustain and unsatisfactory in the long run. Early in the game, in D. H. Lawrence's excentric reading of Freud, the negative load of the castration myth is transformed in the notion of a "first rupture," both "our pain" and "our divinity," centered on "the lotus of the navel," our healed scar, Lawrence's famous solar plexus. Separation between mother and child is a negative rejection, which also includes an "untellable communion of love." Innocently, both become "blind desideratum to the other." Lawrence rejects the corporeal metaphors used by Freud to affirm his "fantasia of the unconscious." As readers, one might retain certain Freudian patterns, an initial deliberate dwelling on the border, a conception of sympton as that which triggers a healing periphrasis. Freud is read, not as a key to the pscyche, or as an exegetical paradigm, but as a modern rewriting of the myths of the psyche. As Harold Bloom points out, the reader of Freud gleans no method which may unlock other readings, but rather an equivocal practice.[3]

By the same token, *De donde* ultimately shakes lose if held to the letter of Lacan, with its emphasis on the role of metaphor and metonymy, on the role of the Phallus as privileged signifier. Such a reading, "in the shadow of a fantastic phallus distributing the lacunae, the passages, and the articulations," would impact Sarduy's text on Lacan's, reducing it to the status of glittering carbuncle encrusted in pachydermic folds.[4] Such false starts are not without value, but they cannot contain a text one of whose recurring motifs is the *danse macabre* of the signifier, its seemingly magnetic pull to the next term, its passage from one to another, away from idealism, including the idealism of the

---

[3] For example, Freud writes that therapy cannot "extirpate" anything, and refers to a "radial penetration," leaving the patient "the work of the periphery," *La Histeria* (Madrid: Alianza, 1967) 194-197. The practice of a "lectura radial," often suggested by Sarduy, is a recurring topos among his readers; for instance, in González Echevarría's various approaches to Sarduy's works. I quote from D. H. Lawrence, *Psychoanalysis of the Unconscious, Fantasia of the Unconscious*, introduction by Philip Rieff (1921, 1922; New York: Viking, 1960) 20-33. See also Harold Bloom, "Freud y lo sublime: una teoría catástrofe de la creatividad," trans. Philip Metzidakis, *Escandalar* 1.1. (1978) 18-30.

[4] Gilles Deleuze, and Félix Guattari, *Anti-Oedipus: Capitalism and Schizophrenia*, trans. R. Hurley, M. Seem. H. R. Lane (Minneapolis: Univ. Minnesota Press, 1977) 97.

signifier: "Da un salto Flor de Loto, y, como el pececillo que al saltar fuera del agua se vuelve colibrí, así vuela entre las lianas" (26). Sarduy's is a difficult text, but it is not obscure. An arcane text may allude to a mystery which cannot be named, but in *De donde* even the mystery of the subject's constitution in language is not alluded to, but written out, opened to a reading.

Among the Nambikwara, who know not of Freud or Lacan, the pointing of the penis at the adversary may be the prelude to war or a peaceful, if edgy, exchange. The significance of such an exchange is less commercial than symbolic. The tribe does not depend on a trade economy; the day after the meeting between the groups, the exchanged objects lie about unnoticed, useful or not as the case might be, but emptied of the significance invested in them during the rite of the day before. It is the women, in the tribe's nomadic search for food, who carry these objects in large baskets, keepers of a discarded symbolic treasure, which subsequent need or chance reinvests with value. The space of the exchange is theatrical, symbolic of the relationship between two distinct groups; it is literally the *theatron,* the seeing place, where the two groups stare at each other, feel, appraise each other's ornaments in an atmosphere of open hostility leading to reciprocal gift-giving. The topos of the theatre as the seeing place of an exchange may be retained and used as another way to approach *De donde son los cantantes,* retained and discarded, to come back to the role of the Nambikwara women, nomadic carriers of the tribe's survival.

All of Sarduy's novel use theatrical motifs. In *Gestos,* the protagonist is a nightclub singer, a born actress who would transform "acting" into "action." Méndez Rodenas convincingly reads the novel as sustained by the contrast between "hacer teatro" and "actuación política," existential opposites in terms of a historical dialectic which is superseded by the protagonist's affirmative "cubanidad," associated with music, popular speech, games of chance, carnival, in short, street theatre, not the historical, tragic, theatre, subverted in turn by the presence of "la mulata."[5] The protagonist in *Gestos* crosses the boundary be-

---

[5] A. Méndez Rodenas, *Severo Sarduy: el neobarroco de la transgresión* (Mexico: Univ. Nacional Autónoma, 1983) 49-100. Subsequent references to the acting/action of the protagonist in *Gestos* draw from this discussion.

tween established theatre, the enclosed place of acting, and her own actions, which are a series of theatrical actions, or rather performances that define her character. One of these is the placing of the bomb, revolutionary action as theatre. Ultimately, the woman's actions, including the placing of the bomb, are informed not by a historical imperative, but by a cultural context whose logic is non-linear and aleatory.

In *De donde son los cantantes,* each of the main narratives has a theatrical setting, the burlesque Shanghai of *Junto al Río,* the "tragedy" of Dolores, which Ulloa cleverly reads as a sort of yoruba operetta,[6] and the carnival/procession of *La Entrada de Cristo.* Theatricality in *Cobra* is discussed in *Relecturas,*[7] and a theatrical setting reappears in the performances of the monks in *Maitreya* and of course in *Colibrí*'s La Casona. Sarduy has written radio scripts and has had the play *La Plage* performed in Europe. If *Gestos* is the passage from historical theatre to the "living theatre" embodied by the protagonist, it is in *De donde son los cantantes* that the theatre as textual conceit is fully developed, creating a pattern, subsequently altered in the other novels, but never abandoned. The novel transforms theatre, the place of seeing, the place of the pallid, "meaningful" Flor, into performance, the *comparsa* of the last section. It transforms the reader from voyeur, the General, "lector baboso," into collaborator in the practice of writing, place of a temporary suspension of the proper name in an classifying activity, in transcription, copy, erasure, addition, deletion.

Theatre in Sarduy's text is a motif so recurring that it may be said to become a controlling image throughout his fictions, which become in turn the symbolic meeting places of two activities: writing/reading. However, narrative is not theatre, and the use of theatrical conceits should be contrasted to the kind of theatre that a writer such as Sarduy has produced. *La playa,* published in *Para la voz* with three other plays,[8] was originally a radioplay

---

[6] Justo C. Ulloa, "Contenido y forma yoruba en 'La Dolores Rondón,'" *Homenaje a Lydia Cabrera* (Miami: Universal, 1978) 245-249.

[7] R. González Echevarría, *Relecturas* (Caracas: Monte Ávila, 1975) 138-139. Characterization in *Maitreya* is discussed in *La ruta de Severo Sarduy* (Hanover, N. H.: Ediciones del Norte, 1987).

[8] *Para la voz* (Madrid: Espiral, 1977).

made of bits of overheard conversations, publicity slogans, sky-writings, all recorded by Sarduy during a visit to Cannes.[9] The play is set on a beach whose props, sunbathers, suntan lotion, lounge chairs, serve as catalysts for the verbal shuffles that make up a text that is memory transformed into discourse. For a listener of the original radioplay, in the right mood, the words flowing out of the receiver must have built a peculiar fantasy, triggered by the play's reverie of words then complemented by the listener's own. The dramatization of the play was something else. In a note on the play, Guy Scarpetta comments on Simone Benmussa's able direction, except where it concerned the actors, who were too "conformist" for the text.[10] In a note on the play originally published in *Le Monde,* Barthes expressed a similar unease with the visual aspects of the play, wishing for "the play of voices," not the "appearance of theatre" (8). The actors were no doubt trained in such a way that, regardless of the text, their facial expressions, their gestures, and particularly their voice expressed a "natural" humanity. The play would have been better suited to the type of performer/actor associated with the Living Theatre or to the dance/performances of such groups as the Polish Mime Theatre; in both, the body and the voice are presented in such way that they demand a different reading; the "humanity" in the voice, in the human body, is not given as something natural, but must be "read" in relation to the script.

The problem with *La Plage*'s 1977 run in Paris was the direction of the actors, whose too solid flesh clashed with the verbal beach fantasies spun in the script. In the program notes, Sarduy wrote that there are no "characters" in the play, but on the stage, the corporeity of the actors, their proper names prominently displayed in the program, was all too apparent, too intrusive. In the texts of Sarduy, the theatrical metaphor works in a non-visual setting, a setting where the specular is itself metaphoric. The dolls in *Cobra* are at times similar to those in the Bunraku theatre, which Barthes mentions as a possible model in his review of Sarduy's play, but the play's actors do not escape the binary

---

[9] "Cronología," *Severo Sarduy* (Madrid: Espiral, 1976) 11.
[10] *Para la voz* 12. The next two references will be made in the text by page number in parenthesis.

banality of the body, not only its binarism, but the weight of a stiff body, incapable of "dancing," to quote Scarpetta quoting Artaud in the introduction to *La playa*. The senile decline of modern theatre is not merely economic, but almost organic, the weight of an old Renaissance body. Sarduy's cultural context is not Renaissance, but Buddhist, baroque, pre-Colombian, all of which implies a different body, one not fixed on a sexual identity, a fragmented, shifting body (9-11).

The kind of writing projected in *De donde* is based on a theatrical metaphor whose support is the body, not the masked body of Renaissance theatre, but the performing body of the transvestite, coloquially, and more appropriately, the "drag queen"; for the transvestite, or the crossdresser, may limit his actions to the hysterical solitude of a hotel room, sometimes away from wife and family, while the drag queen is always a performer, and always a performer with a self-endowed name. Among the less imaginative drags, the name may be a copy or a composite of a star's name, Liza, Liz, Marilyn, or Diana LaRue. Among the drag literati, it may be an allusion to a favorite character: Erishia Dubois. Others give freeplay to the phonology of the exotic: Elite Chanson, Channelle Fontainne, Erika VonCourt, Francesa Wakeland. Few are unabashedly deconstructive: Charlene Buns, or Kissa Myass.[11] Without the intensity of Artaud, the performance of the drag queen implicitly questions the limits of representation and initiates a pact with the audience. It is the structure of that pact, and not the repetitive trappings of crossdressing, that may serve as a model for the kind of writing unleashed in *De donde son los cantantes*, and which comes to constitute in Sarduy's

---

[11] These "drag" names belong to performers I have seen in North Carolina. I refer to men dressing as women because the complementary phenomenon, woman as man, as way of life and performance, though not uncommon, has to be "read" differently; in some cases, a woman can dress like a man, and not only pass, but enhance her allure, a tradition which brings to mind such names as Garbo or Dietrich. On the other hand, the transgression of the male crossdresser always has an element of aggression and disruption. Distinguishing between the transvestite and the transexual, Sarduy writes "Para el travestí, la dicotomía y oposición de los sexos queda abolida o reducida a criterios inoportunos o arqueológicos; para el transexual, al contrario, esa oposición no sólo se mantiene sino que es subrayada, aceptada: simplemente el sujeto, tomando el 'corte' al pie de la letra, ha saltado del otro lado de la barra." *La simulación* (Caracas: Monte Ávila, 1982) 65.

subsequent works, not an ideology of inversion, gayness or homosexuality, but a style, an attitude within language, at once pragmatic and derisive, *de risa,* a movement which overflows the very subject it has aimed to constitute, which does not rest on the wistful subjectivity of writer/reader as possessors of the one sign whose ambiguity is never in question: the proper name.

If in Saussure's *Cours,* writing is not the "vestment" but the "travestissement" of speech, if speech is "natural" and writing a perverse afterthought, the writer has two choices: embrace the travesty or write in the nostalgia of a primal speech. In *De donde son los cantantes,* Auxilio and Socorro, the subject's beloved agents, like the two-headed bat on the Bacardi bottle, look both ways, tug at both sides of the Saussurean split between speech and writing. The tapestry-sign, says Socorro, has (oral) meaning, "lengua de Mortal hay en ellos" (97). For Auxilio, on the other hand, the tapestry is to be a prized token in a metonymic commerce akin to writing, "Vendido sería nuestra fortuna, empeñado casa y cocido, negociado en los telares de Almería la más espesa de las joyas" (97), writing as a chiseled, opaque artifact.

The splitting of the tapestry is the "climax" of the novel, if such a word is accurate in this case, the high point in Freytag's Pyramid of rising and falling action, leading to a catastrophe, the bullets rained on the pair at the end. Such a dramatic scheme would hold if the confrontation between Auxilio and Socorro were of a moral, existential order, if the novel moved toward some sort of resolution, however catastrophic. Yet as in the ancient authorless fables, the text says, "It was, and it was not,"[12] as opposed to the modern novel's dialectics of choice. For the possibility of such a choice rests with an authority on the periphery of the text, signalled by the proper name. The *Nota* at the end of *De donde son los cantantes* is the farewell to that name, the farewell to "Los monólogos de Dolores," so centered in Camagüey, in her role as poet "saved" from the dead by a few lines of verse. In the *Nota,* "Este hombre es el mismo," cast in the tense commerce of the letter.

---

[12] Roman Jakobson, "Linguistics and Poetics," *The Structuralists: From Marx to Lévi-Strauss,* ed. Richard and Fernande DeGeorge (Garden City, N.Y.: Doubleday, 1972) 112.

In a way correlative to the drag queen's sacrifice of her proper name for the sake of an exotic moniker (her theatrical marking), the writing subject in *De donde* throws down the onomastic gauntlet, never to retrieve it again. By the time the father in *Colibrí* tells "Severo" to stop burning papers, because among "los Sarduy, hasta ahora, no ha habido ningún pájaro," it is too late.[13] Sarduy's name, on the advertising periphery of *De donde son los cantantes,* has already been sucked into the text. It could appear in a thousand autobiographies, and it would ever ring like the broken bell in the monk's temple. It has been emptied in/by/through writing, and it demands, perversely, compassionately, no less of the reader. But the exchange is guaranteed, the excentric affirmation of a leap without nets, the possibility of a world of signs, without truth, without origin, ever offered to interpretation, to the switching and rearranging of given pieces. The strange commerce of the Nambikwara correlates to their use of the proper name; they forbid its use, forcing the intruder to use "borrowed" names. To give out someone's name is an assault on that person.[14] In *De donde son los cantantes,* the portrait of the ancestors, "el retrato de los antepasados," recedes in "la penumbra de los interiores," along with "los bruñidos relojes, los espejos, las opulentas copas de piña," the waning of *lo cubano,* Vitier, Lezama.[15] In its place, rather, over its place, for once inscribed nothing is entirely erased, there surges a signature: "una omega de tiza, dos peces opuestos y unidos por un hilo. O quizás una firma" (125). It is an allusion to the proper of the name banished from the text, the one motivated sign lost and wasted in writing.

It is the motivation of the proper name in relation to its referent, the person carrying the name, that is unraveled in *De*

---

[13] (Barcelona: Argos Vergara, 1984) 129.
[14] *Tristes tropiques* 315-318.
[15] *La ruta de Severo Sarduy* 65-68. González Echevarría reads *De donde* as a "*deslectura*" of Lezama and Carpentier. He also finds in the four parts of the *Curriculum* a pattern analogous to the fourfold *bakongo* cosmogram, which serves as a model for the "signatures" of secret societies in the Afro-Cuban cult. Following this path, he suggests that the *Nota* is the tail, the curlicue, at the end of such a signature (122-131). Approaching the novel from the point of view of the elided subject, it may be read as an extended "signature," a simulacrum of the name of the signer on the periphery of the text. The name of the man, transformed into a common name, having lost its proper, pales before the richly inscribed patterns of a textual signature.

donde son los cantantes. When the Narrators argue in *La Dolores Rondón*, they argue over the motivation of the sign in relation to the object named. For them "el perro" is "la palabra," and their argument alludes to the French version of a familiar proverb – "His bark is worse than his bite," "Perro que ladra no muerde," and "Le mot *chien* ne mord pas."[16] Their arguments preface the existential identity crisis of Dolores and alludes to Sartre's division between the words of the prose writer, those which "signify," and those of the poets, whose words contain "meaning," words as pointers in prose, words as things in poetry. Dolores may be doomed by the prosaic Narrators' insistence on the linearity of her story, but she thinks she is saved because she is after all a poet, her verses sculpted in stone. For the writing subject in *De donde son los cantantes*, the Sartrean opposition, privileging the poetic word in its "natural" motivation, does not hold. The illusory totality achieved by Dolores, whose life is centered on her one masterpiece, belongs to death even before her story begins. Her story is the story of a corpse, for what the book-tombstone delivers is a dead totality, a sequel to the awaited corpse of Flor in *Junto al Río*, redolent with potential meaning for the duped General. The gesture of writing, its caress, is lost when the book is born, printed, bound, and gagged like Donoso's *imbunche*. Yet the final distingretion of Mortal suggests the possibility of another corpus, fragmented, pieced together, simulacrum of the gesture of the hand in writing, inscription and call, never safe in the peaceful intersubjectivity of mutual affirmations, but rather erotic summoning, beyond irony, to a dangerous cruise. In *De donde son los cantantes*, the theatre is a degraded space, the shoddy rehearsals of El Director, the histrionics of Dolores; both are the place of Artaud's dreaded "repetitions." In *De donde son los cantantes*, the "theatre" is transformed into the scene of writing; its pale double is the scene of reading.

The burlesque theatre in *Junto al Río* becomes the focus of the General's metaphysical hunger. He is content to see Flor strut her hour upon the stage over and over, and can only stop the repetition with the deadly bracelet. His theatre is strictly the

---

[16] Gérard Genette, *Mimologiques* (Paris: Seuil, 1976) 9. Subsequently, I draw from Genette's discussion of Sartre's *Qu'est-ce que la littérature?* (295-302).

seeing place, specular, narcissistic, monologic, for the General can only be tricked into dealing with Auxilio and Socorro, whose travesty of Flor he refuses to accept. As he waits in his store, which holds "el resto," everything that Flor is not, he refuses a system of references other than Flor.[17] Through negation, Flor, the object of the metaphysical closure of representation, manifests herself, allows herself to be seen by the voyeuristic General. As he waits for the corpse, he waits on the threshold of meaning, the guilded carrot dangled before his "cirrosis ontológica." In the next section, the "essence" of Flor reincarnates in fleshy Dolores, who along with Mortal, plays out her hard-headed, univocal role, also in a degraded theatrical setting parcelled out by the dialectic Narrators. The triadic Auxilio-Socorro-Clemencia are her attendants, but it is also they who reintroduce the plural wisdom of numbers.

In *La Entrada de Cristo,* theatre turns into *comparsa,* and the drama is played in Mortal's body, pieced together by the semiotic pair and dragged through the symbolic landscape. The dancing disintegration of Mortal as a figure of the writing subject may be read, part of the way at least, in light of Artaud's remarks on the theatre.[18] Artaud's theatre of cruelty begins with the erasure of the name of man, with the flight from the metaphysical enclosure of representational theatre, with the transformation of the body into theatre. Representational theatre is built on repetition, "rehearsal" in French; it is a theological space dominated by the spoken word, the breath of life being given to the printed words of a memorized script, issued from a distant "author-creator."

As in the Western theatre described by Barthes, what is seen on the stage hides the concept of the soul. Even less than the illusion of reality, what this type of theatre projects is the illusion of totality. The caricature of the puppet, a phallic chip off the old block (the human actor), parodically underlines the phantasmagoric wholeness of the body erected behind the proscenium arch

---

[17] Mikhail Bakhtine, *La poétique de Dostoievski,* trans. I. Kolitcheff (Paris: Seuil, 1970) 69. Bakhtin writes that in spite of the polyphonic quality of the Baroque theatre, "le drame théâtral est étranger à une polyphonie authentique; il peut avoir des plans multiples mais non des *mondes multiples,* il n'admet qu'un seul système de référence."

[18] I base the following remarks about Artaud on J. Derrida, "Le théâtre de la cruauté et la clôture de la représentation," *L'écriture et la différence* 341-368.

of the theatre. Artaud's parricidal gesture would rob the theatre of its ontological center, the Saussurean holy alliance between the spoken word and, in a supporting, but no less essential, role, the written word of the script. Artaud consigns the word to the margin, puts it in its place, and insists on the primacy of other theatrical "gestures."

In his "madness," Artaud opts for a new kind of theatrical "writing," a new grammar including spoken language and writing, but also other plastic, visual elements, transforming characters into "hieroglyphs" which may be said to reproduce the workings of the Freudian dream; however, Artaud's is an ordered, "cruel" dream, and he distances himself from the lurking idealism of the Freudian unconscious. Artaud's "cruel" theatre is the realm of surfaces, a photosensitive surface exposed to a merciless highnoon glare, without possible substitute, played but once, murdering God and man, erasing their names. Artaud's rejection of repetition is a rejection of writing. His project for the theatre has had practical repercussions in contemporary theatre, but no followers, for ultimately it is his own body that is sacrificed in the purity of its difference. His project has come closest to being fulfilled by conceptual artists and performers who have skirted mutilation and death in an attempt to flee the repetetive phantasmagoria of representation.

De donde son los cantantes may be theatrical, or rather performative; but it is neither theatre nor performance. It is condemned to a peculiar distance. It is, *faute de mieux,* a fable of representation. Flor de Loto, Signified, Object, is the corpse of representation, put forth by her slave-interpreters, Auxilio-Socorro, intermittently obedient to an unseen master, whom they betray nonetheless at every turn. Flor is offered to the General, who is all eyes. She is the gilded death mask of the *modernistas,* an apparition from Darío's "Página Blanca," "la Pálida,/ la vestida de ropas obscuras,/ la Reina invencible, la bella inviolada:/ la Muerte." Like Darío's "bella inviolada," Sarduy's Flor is "la Emperatriz," "casta y pura," "una máscara blanca." Dolores, like the protagonist in *Gestos,* is the existential heroine who wants to wed acting to action, to make artifice, her wigs and her dancing, legitimate by pushing toward power, "¡El poder está en las caderas!" "¡Calva, coja, pero a La Habana!" (74-75). She heads for the deadly tautologies of the Narrators, "todo vuelve al todo,"

"Es decir a la nada" (87). Mortal is the author-god resurrected to play out in his own body, like Artaud, a moveable, non-repetitive "feast of cruelty"; the spectators lined along the way see a different figure with every step, a new non-repetitive stage of his decomposition. The General, Dolores, Mortal, are personified writing gestures meeting in *De donde son los cantantes,* which is nevertheless not the sum of its parts; rather, it is the anatomy of all those writing gestures. Artaud's corporeal apotheosis may have its simulacrum in Mortal's dancing exit, but Artaud's corporeal metaphysics is more than once removed from writing as a process which is by definition repetitive and ludicrous, older than all the ontologies it has served, even that of the body, unoriginal, and archaic.

2: PARTING GLANCES

In "Tu dulce nombre halagará mi oído," an introduction to a volume dedicated to Gertrudis Gómez de Avellaneda, Sarduy refers to the privilege accorded in Cuban tradition to the "whispered word," which precedes the image. He writes of a name whose call is felt bodily, a sign which calls, and touches us: "Los cubanos conocemos muy bien ese llamado corporal del nombre, signo que más que interpelarnos, nos toca, chisporroteo más vívido y presente que la imagen, más próximo al rumor de la tierra." Sarduy's Lezamian nostalgia, however, comes back around to the printed word. The space of the proffered word, he writes, lingered into our century, sustained by "curiosity" and by the printing press, "los honores locales de la imprenta." The sound of the spoken word comes to Sarduy's generation, a generation that publishes, already as a curious echo or as print: "Los que comenzamos a publicar en los años cincuenta lo conocimos aún."[1] It may be said that Sarduy is poised in a spot analogous to the "tense polarity" of the Baroque, between a proffered word, "the ecstacy of the creature," and the written, printed word, "the composure of the creature," between the delicious hysteria of Dolores, on one side, and the scriptural mastery of the writing subject on the other.[2] However, Sarduy is not a Baroque writer in this sense. His polarities are not as

---

[1] *Homenaje a Gertrudis Gómez de Avellaneda* 19-21.
[2] Walter Benjamin, *The Origin of German Tragic Drama*, trans. John Osborne (London: NLB, 1977) 201.

"tense" as they are porous; they are merrily schizoid, in the popular sense of the word, off-beat, off-the-wall.

In Sarduy's comments, the visual image is preceded by a whispered word, a privileged sequence which passed on to a written tradition. For la Avellaneda, Cuba was "dulce nombre," "nombre divino," but Sarduy also points to her formalism, at times heavyhanded, "trabajo de orfebrería." From this not so improbable encounter between Severo and Gertrudis, three terms are retained: image/sound/inscription, or looking/naming/writing. All three refer to modes of representation whose crises constitute another twist in the adventures of *De donde son los cantantes*. In the Baroque, the "temporal incompatability" of voice and look prefaces the subject's alternate expression. Such an expression, a subjective unfolding, is ironic, parodic.[3] By contrast, the subject in *De donde son los cantantes* transforms that irony in order to bracket representational pretensions. A backward glance at the outlines of such bracketing may substitute for a more systematic summary.

Junto al Río is the looking place; there are eyes everywhere, a movie house, mural paintings, and of course the burlesque theatre. It is the place of seeing which turns the pursuit of the voyeuristic General into an ordeal. The figure of Flor oscillates between disguise and presence, between the string of names manipulated by Auxilio and Socorro and Flor's expected arrival as pure representation, framed by the proscenium of the theatre. In his mock-Dantesque descent, the General enters a smelly basement where damp spots on the wall turn out to be a fresco, depicting Auxilio, Socorro, and Carita as monks who paint/write. The General has to go through the painting, finds the deceiving Director, hears a Lacanian litany on the "being of birds," and is declared cured by the "exmandarina." The enigmatic speech of the skinny Chinese, sidekick of the Director, presents a series of transformations:

> –El ser de los pájaros no es el timbre del trino, sino las plumas cayendo a cada muda. Blancas, son otro pájaro en la nieve, la firma del primero; rojas, pez que se vuelve mariposa

---

[3] José Muñoz Millares, "El 'concepto' de la alegoría," *Linguistica e Letteratura* 6.2 (1981): 117.

si lo atacan. Otro cuando muda, despista dejando ojillos de
culebra entre las viejas plumas: dota de mirada a su impostura;
su júbilo es clavarse en el aire frente a su doble ciego, enfrentar
a los tigres del apócrifo. ¡Oh, ardientes!
¡Oh, feroces!
¡Oh, dulces pájaros! (48)

The passage is not as obscure as it is knotty, a nodal spot in the text. From the "being of birds," a metonymic reverie leads to a confrontation with a duplicity whose outlines are defined in the process. The suggestiveness of the passage will survive even a crude paraphrase, which may read as follows: The "being" of the writing subject, who may be a "pájaro"/Cuban queen, is not substantially in him, in his voice ("trino"/warbling), however sweet it may sound, nor is it exclusively threefold, dependent on a trinitarian (peircean, lacanian, heideggerian) model of the sign ("timbre del trino"/ sign of the threefold). The duping of the General and Dolores depends on such a sign, incarnated in Auxilio-Socorro. The subject passes through the trinitarian model, the realms of the General and Dolores, but the activity of writing is the backward retracing of such a passage, its unraveling. The decomposition of Mortal-Christ, privileged and degraded third party, is the fiction of this necessary undoing. Furthermore, the subject's proper is not in his name, the sign whose propriety would remain unquestioned, but in the marks that he leaves, "las plumas cayendo a cada muda." Even if these marks are white on white, they always rely on another subject, who returns to the first his "signature," "la firma del primero." These marks may be of another sort, red for example, but their result is always metonymic displacement, a bird which turns into a butterfly. The subject, now "Otro," leaves marks which are false eyes among the feathers he discarded, his "first" marks. In this way, the subject gives his false double a way of looking, "dota de mirada a su impostura." The joy of the writing/marking subject is to confront his "blind" double and give him the (fictitious) possibility of "looking," of obliquely confronting the potential other's passions, "enfrentar a los tigres del apócrifo." Correlatively, it may be said that commentary also must pass through a trinitarian phase, Peirce's pragmatic model of the sign in which the last term is habit, the habit of commentary, but in the long run, perhaps commentary turns into the anamorphic double of the text, the erasure of another proper name.

In "Du regard," Lacan elaborates on the constitution of the subject by asking a question about a painting bird, which would paint by dropping its feathers, as a snake its scales, or a tree its leaves. The anecdote corresponds to his references to the mimetic gestures of certain butterflies whose eye-like markings, "ocelles," perhaps "fascinate" predators, which may lead one to think that such fascination is peculiar to eyes, imitated by the eye-like markings. However, the opposite may be true: that eyes themselves fascinate because they are like markings, like the "ocelles" on the wings of butterflies. The anecdote serves to distinguish "eyes" from "looking," the space of the subject. The look is his realm. He paints to leave a gesture, to replay that look, evident even in trompe l'oeil.

Some critics have pointed to the perverse limitations of the work of American hyperrealist sculptor Duane Hanson, who has made polyvinyl, deceivingly lifelike replicas of ordinary folk: a weary K-Mart shopper, a repairman, a motel maid. The viewer of such sculptures, however, need not dwell on the limitations; his pleasure comes from the contrast between the image of the weary shopper and its possible double. In *La simulación,* Sarduy writes that the viewer of a Hanson lookalike creates a trompe-l'oeil square, the confrontation, on an equal footing, of the object and its simulacrum: "en que no hay jerarquía en lo verosímil, es decir, prioridad ontológica."[4]

In nature, the eye-like markings on the wings of butterflies may deceive, but our eyes have a lethal, aggressive function; the Lacanian subject looks to be looked at. One may recall the aggressive stares of the Nambikwara, a prelude to the edgy,

---

[4] *La simulación* (Caracas: Monte Ávila, 1982) 46-47. Sarduy does not mention Duane Hanson, but he is obviously describing one of his sculptures, "Una matrona americana, de cera pintada, se reposa un momento recostada a la pared..." Hanson's works are not, however, "painted wax," but polyvinyl molds, polychromed in oil; the accesories, and even some of body hair, may be real. Sarduy goes on to describe another Hanson work, the Bowery bums; significantly, he ends up describing what may be their dream, "sueñan, quizás"; the dream is an erotic encounter between a boy and a woman, joined by a line of semen, "sólo ese trazo los une." It is as if Sarduy inserted this description, possibly of another painting, in the "dream" of the life-like Bowery bum. In such insertions, he plays out "un goce mayor," beyond the trompe-l'oeil of the sculptures.

symbolic exchange of goods. In *De donde son los cantantes* the General replays the agression of that stare. He wants to "look at" Flor without understanding that he cannot constitute his self in this way. He's a "gallinita ciega" (41) before Flor; at the same time, the eyes ("ojillos") looking through the cracks allude to the peering writing subject. Sarduy's "birds" do not merely shed their feathers; they move metonymically toward a confrontation with a blind double. In this way, a subjective relationship is defined which is a far cry from the whining objections of the Unamunesque "Lector" included in the novel.

Yet *De donde son los cantantes* is not the specular space of a painting, although it may cite such a space; visually, it is limited to the contrast of black letters on yellowing paper. The novel would transform such a limitation into a possibility. When in "Una nueva versión de los hechos" Auxilio doubles up, "cuerpo con su reflejo," to produce the General, his appearance as a character coincides with that of "yo," by this point a degraded repository of subjectivity whose first appearance includes the reference to Lacan's "painting bird." Since Auxilio gets stuck to the General, Socorro suggests that the General remove his coat. "Yo" replies, "–Hija mía, ¿no ves que si el general se quita sus quincallas sería como el pájaro pintor de Lacan que se quita sus plumas'" (19). When Lacan discusses the relationship between painting and the position of this elided subject, he suggests that representation in painting is always illusory. The spots left by a painter mark the end of a gesture, and the painting "traps" the viewer, who looks in vain for the "eyes" in those gestural marks. As subject in the economy of desire, the painter may reproduce an image, but that is ancillary to his participation in a different sort of pact in which there is no thing in itself; there is the look (95). We are spared the business of distinguishing between this thing in itself and the subject. There is what D. H. Lawrence calls "unconscious subjectivity," negative in its "blind rejection" and positive as the "untellable communion of love."[5]

The General desires Flor and searches for her in a theatrical space, through a space where someone paints. He is "fascinated" by Flor – *fascinum* means evil eye, jinx, charm, amulet, penis.

---

[5] *Psychoanalysis and the Unconscious* (1921; New York: Viking, 1960) 29.

Flor is his thing, and she is irrevocably lost. Duly punished, his nail pulled off, the General is saddled with the symbolic Auxilio-Socorro; still, he would "fix" Flor with his evil eye. However, it is the General himself who is fixed in a constant watch, "Centinela en su almena." He fails to recognize his own elision, the removal of his coat/feathers, which would be equivalent to an admission of a dependence on the doubling Auxilio-Socorro. The General does not accept the fact that Flor, like the murderous bracelet, is "algo en apariencia muy banal" (53), that in the metaphysical theatre he enters, and in the text we read, all is residue, juxtaposition of sullied sediments, recycled excreta, peddled by Literature from the day one. Trapped in the theatre, the General is caught in its one-way street, cut off from it and not willing to defer communication, the arrival of Flor. The text cites the theatrical space, its sad "unidirectional relationship," but it asks of the reader "the willing suspension of disbelief," the deferral of a ready communication for the tracing of a different sort of subjectivity, less theatrical, yet more participatory.[6] The General's plight is the plight of the humanist in the exploded electric plant of modernity, and points to a current pedagogical impasse in the collegiate incarnation of the so-called liberal arts: how to teach students avid to find a productive role in a competitive marketplace that literature is an empty hoax, but one we could do with, that at its best it embodies the value and the weight *(el peso)* of language, before going the way of the sundry ideologies it inevitably and faithfully serves. *De donde son los cantantes* aims to teach us to feel that weight, and to treasure it.

During the discussion period after Lacan's comments on the "evil eye," François Wahl asks if there is a "good eye," a "prophylactic" one, as in the Mediterranean cultures, one which would have a protective function, linked not to castration's aggressive stoppage, but to a movement, a duration. Lacan answers that all human desire is based on castration and that the eye takes from it its lethal function; it is not a decoy, as it is in nature, the "eyes" on the wings of butterflies he mentions earlier. Wahl's question suggests that the narrative, "un certain trajet," may offer such a prophylactic "eye," against the virulence and

---

[6] Roberto Echavarren, "On Literariness," 86.

agression of the evil eye and its castrating legacy. At any rate, the space of writing is only metaphorically specular; its "eye" is shattered, perhaps not free of the virulence of the specular, but aiming for another rapport, linked not to a stop, to death, but to a movement. The text may have the same function as Wahl's amulet: "a protective function during a certain trajectory, which is bound not to stoppage, but to movement."[7] The General's loss is another man's (relative) comfort. The Sarduy subject, supported by the scavenging pair, takes the consequences and makes of writing the legible arrangement of that sullage; it moves away from the realm of the evil eye, of the *fascinum*, turning the book into a protective amulet, one of those minutely phallic *azabaches* pinned to Cuban babies in the heydey of the pseudo-republic, folk prophylactic, effective at least for the duration of a reading, sane in that way. Now one recalls the role of the ant-like Nambikwara women who gather the objects discarded by the men after their tense exchange and carry them in baskets, to be taken out when necessary. The physical and spiritual survival of the tribe depends no less on their nomadic trajectory, during which those exchanged objects are used, than on the men's aggressive, symbolic ritual of exchange. I am not suggesting that there is something "primitive" in the working of the text, but that it may be read in light of a pattern evident in the customs of the Nambikwara, a pattern of symbolic exchange/deferred violence/ movement/ revaluation/ survival.

If *Junto al Río* is the undoing of a representational drive founded on looking, reflections, mirrors, theatre, *La Dolores Rondón* picks up the pieces and adds another layer, representation as a crisis of naming. In Foucault's reading of *Las Meninas*, he writes that in the space where the painting is seen, "the observer and the observed take part in a ceaseless exchange."[8] The proper names of the figures in the painting may be "useful landmarks," but they only affirm that words and images may not be reduced to each other's terms; they belong to realms that do

---

[7] *Les quatre concepts fondamentaux de la psychanalyse*. Wahl points out that there may a "prophylactic" eye: "Il a une fonction de protection qui dure pendant un certain trajet, et qui est liée, non pas à un arrêt, mais à un mouvement," 108. The translation of this sentence in the text is mine.

[8] *The Order of Things* (New York: Random House, 1970) 4-5. Subsequent references in the text by page number in parenthesis.

not translate into each other, realms which posit "an infinite relation" (9). A picture is never worth a thousand words, or one, or a million, not because one is inferior or superior to the other, but because words function in another order: "the space where they achieve their splendour is not that deployed by our eyes but that defined by the sequential elements of syntax" (9). The unfolding crisis that is the Baroque mourns the loss of that "splendour," and takes it out on the syntax, on its soiled black/white innocence. Its metaphor covers an elided name and grandly mimics the gesture of pointing, the propriety/property of the name.

In *De donde* the deictic illusion is unhinged in order to sustain another relation between looking and naming, in order to undermine the pointed finger of metaphor, pointed at the proper of the name. Remember that in Guillén's poem, the father's finger pointed the way, forced the poet to "speak": "Me obligan/ el perfil de mi padre, su índice de recuerdo/no puedo hablar, pero me llaman/ su detenida voz y el sollozo del viento."[9] For the perambulating poet, provincial *flâneur*, the reward is the luminous image of the mother in the window, *"y de sus ojos, que son/ojos de suave paloma,/latiendo de nuevo, toma/nueva luz mi corazón."* In Guillén: Silence/patriarchal pointing/metaphor/poetic voice/luminous maternal image. In *De donde* those slashes, if upheld, would be insurmountable barriers; the relationship of language to vision cannot follow the redeeming trajectory written out in Guillén's "elegía camagüeyana." Instead, the subject resides in those slashes, porous tilted membranes. The proper of the name is erased, in order to affirm what Foucault calls "the infinity of the task" (10). Like the General in his visual apotheosis, Dolores is duped in her eponymous glory. Her "bombast" is a linguistic gesture of recuperation, her way of easing Benjamin's "tense polarity" between the graphic and the phonic.[10] She is the heroine of a Cratylian reverie, where the Narrators talk of "toothless" words, "barking" words, words invested with an essence mirrored in the name of Dolores, a sad pointer to the body buried somewhere in Camagüey.

---

[9] "Elegía camagüeyana," *Obra poética, 1920-1958*, 2 vols. (La Habana: Instituto Cubano del Libro, 1972) 1: 410-416.
[10] *The Origin of German Tragic Drama* 201.

The ideal unity of that body dissolves on the printed page; correlatively, the ideal unity of the name, Dolores/Serolod/ Severo/O revés, disintegrates on that page, in its black/ white spacing: her illusory wholeness fades when the precision of the visual comes into question. Near the end, Dolores recalls "los ojos desvelados como entonces" (82). Desvelado: sleepless, but also a common Gallicism for "discovered," "unveiled," "unmasked." "Los ojos desvelados" are the eyes whose veils have lifted, whose "mystery" floats on to the page, becoming blind *eye* to a "doble ciego," ineluctable modality of the graphic. Dialectical to the end, Dolores trusts her words carved in stone, "Para que te acuerdes de mí te dejo estas palabras" (83). She is doomed along with the Oedipal Mortal, whose feet swell, "algo donde meter estos pies que crecen, que se hinchan" (81). The two define their own fearful symmetry. When Auxilio and Socorro throw away the pan where Mortal has washed his aching feet, something like throwing the baby out with the bath water, the sound "repeats" the noise made by the pots and pans triumphantly thrown into the street by Dolores, *"¡Previsible simetría!"* (81). What the textual undoing of such dualities leaves behind is sullage, residue, traces left by the writer, successive juxtaposition of tiny deposits, orebody, miner's payload.

In *Junto al Río* and *La Dolores* two representations are deferred, Flor on the burlesque stage, Dolores in her "living" drama. The first relies on the General's libidinous, piercing eyes; the second, on the wilful orality of Dolores. The sequence from one tale to the next dramatizes the incompatability of Foucault's "what we see" and "what we say," which in any case is not "what we get." This incompatability prefaces the alternative space of *La Entrada de Cristo,* the realm where the insular orality of the pair, literally spread out in the tropical cathedral, becomes the realm of the printed letter: "Desde la tribuna los fieles les tiraban puñados de bolas negras que se abrían en el aire: flores de seda china. Quedaban flotando: jardines negros. Caían; en los pétalos, incompleto, al revés, impreso Su nombre, roto" (143) - "Incompleto, al revés" spells "séver"; Is "sever" part of "Su nombre, roto," part of "severo"? It may be a severed part, sever-o graphically sever-ed. Sarduy comments on the use of the anagram as lair of the proper name in "El barroco y el neobarroco." He writes of a writing inside writing, "escritura entre la escritura," and refers to the possibility of reading something other that what is offered by the linear order of the printed page: "Las líneas tipográficas, paralelas y regulares." Such a reading finds other connections; it involves a different doing, the deferral of meaning and the focusing on the specificity of the letter. The anagram, hiding place and showcase of the name, calls attention to this graphic specificity: "operación por excelencia del escondite onomástico."[11]

The Baroque "desengaño" centers on the failure of representation, on the letter's aggressive superimposition on the ideal promise of things. The subject's representational failure traps him, "deflates" him, catches him between two mutually exclusive gestures: naming and looking. Yet in the Baroque concept of allegory, an "ironic ambivalence saves the *I*, relatively speaking," the *I* as producer of the signifier, lame, degraded, whose very sense is the absence of the desired object.[12] In *De donde son los cantantes,* the cutting of the allegorical tapestry signals an alteration, a move toward a different, if not a new, order, aimed beyond the loss of the object and the subject's renunciation of representation, beyond a subject caught in the act, saved by the ironic bell. The cutting of the tapestry signals the unraveling of irony and the possible bracketing of desire, the transformation of the "melancholy" of its loss, a brave new retooling of *desengaño.*

Gazing at someone carries the implicit expectation that our look will be returned; Benjamin's "aura" is experienced when the look is returned, when "the expectation is met": "to perceive the aura of an object we look at means to invest it with the ability to look at us in return."[13] The "inhuman" camera, specially the old box camera, demands a sustained gaze from the poser, a gaze which is not returned. The production of the image depends on a distant gesture, the mechanical clic of the objective manipulated by the hand of the photographer; hence the spell cast by the fixed image, the record of a gaze not returned, blindly looking at us. That is perhaps the fascination of photographs, whether Kertész

---

[11] "El barroco y el neobarroco," *América latina en su literatura,* ed. César Fernández Moreno (Mexico: Siglo XXI, 1972) 178.

[12] Muñoz Millanes 95-96.

[13] Walter Benjamin, *Charles Baudelaire: a Lyric poet in the Era of High Capitalism,* trans. Harry Zohn (London: NLB, 1973) 147. Subsequent references in the text.

or Arbus, or the homey polaroids; they have what Barthes calls "the Look."[14] If a painting such as *Las Meninas* opens a specular space, reconstituted in Baroque poetry, the angles that defined such a space are subsequently refracted. With Baudelaire, writes Benjamin, the eyes "have lost their ability to look" (149). Left to its own devices, *De donde son los cantantes,* like the General, may also be a "gallinita ciega," full of glazed, neon eyes, in heavily made-up sockets. One may wish that a critical gesture could animate such an object, could "invest it with the ability to look at us in return" (148). But that may be asking too much.

For the Baroque poet the sun dial is an allegory of the visible, and a model of writing: it "records the movement of a glance during the present. In the same way that the pen, tracing the white page, leaves a mark, fixed by the letter, of the temporal discontinuity of perception, the dial is the sun's accountant, leaving a record, in shadow, of the falling of light, of its fugacity."[15] Even Stephen Dedalus considers the "ineluctable modality of the visible/ ineluctable modality of the audible/ Signature of all things I am here to read."[16] For him, if not for Joyce, "The sun is there, the slender trees, the lemon houses" (42). The irony Stephen/Joyce is a familiar replay. One may recall that, false son to a false father, Hamlet says he is too much in the sun. He is already cast from light; his real father has been transformed into a lightless, "extravagant" "illusion." He is left before the usurper and his perfidious mother with a poor pun. Since then, light has been of another sort, the "merciless glare" that blinds the myopic, ludicrous, visionary Blanche Dubois at the bowling alley. In *De donde son los cantantes,* after *"(Black out),"* Auxilio and Socorro cry, "¡No! Somos la Luz. Simplemente nos hemos convertido en su ausencia. Ahora somos sus islas. ¡Mira!" (42). Later they manifest themselves as "Luz fría. Sí, un gran neón circular ilumina el reservado" (44). In *De donde son los cantantes* the outlines of the letter blur in a hazy, artificial light, lacunae of the visible, radical distance from what Sarduy calls "los dos ejes

---

[14] *Camera Lucida: Reflections on Photography,* trans. Richard Howard (New York: Hill and Wang, 1981) 114.
[15] Muñoz Millanes 101. The translation of the phrase is mine.
[16] *Ulysses* (1914, 1918; New York: Modern Library, 1961) 37. The next reference, given in the text, is to this edition.

epistémicos del siglo barroco: el dios – el verbo de potencia infinita – jesuita, y su metáfora terrestre, el rey,"[17] radical distance also from the metonymy of god and king, the father, the pointing, ordering father of Guillén's poem. In Sarduy, he would be transformed into accomplice in a ritual akin to crossdressing, ludicrous, purging mimicking of the absent mother, loving raid of her box of trinkets, work of a subject possessed not by duality, father/son, father/mother, man/woman, homo/hetero, gay/straight, but by a feigning drive, distance from the sun dial in the topiary garden, distance from the tropical sun, from an ironic recuperation, slim possibility, however, of a circuitous rescue.

For the contemporary writer in a lethal consumer economy, self-promotion has gone hand in hand with writing. The promotion of a marketable self, ground in the myth of the individual, has paralleled the terrifying privacy of a writing activity where individuality shatters and the letter emerges in all its pathos, and all its power. The dilemma is hardly new. Darío, who understood the devastating clash between public persona and scriptural subject, saw it lucidly. Macedonio Fernández writes of the author's photographs on the cover of a book, "¡Qué caras seguras y felices las de esas tapas!"[18] He refers to the man whose smile reveals "un profesional de la felicidad." The toothy publicitary grins of some contemporary writers come to mind. In his photographs Sarduy seems to frown or to look away from the camera, recalling Auxilio's look when one of the Narrators reminds her of "la espiral del tiempo del ser": *"lo mira con el rabo de los ojos, que prolonga una línea de oro."* The visage that emerges from Sarduy's own flirt with stardom, recorded in interviews, photographs, and video, contrasts with a face in the text which is blank, like the face of the man who openly moves the dolls in the Bunraku theatre of Japan. For the writer, there is always time, and with the fading of the public image, the future promises a new image, Bakhtin's "special type of image," ever restored by the power of the letter,[19] not literary visage, persona, on mask but *visaje,* a gesture and a movement, a face, as in "he made a face." *De*

---

[17] "El barroco y el neobarroco" 183.

[18] Macedonio Fernández, "Una novela que comienza," *Manera de una psique sin cuerpo* (Barcelona: Tusquets, 1973) 35.

[19] *Speech Genres and Other Late Essays,* trans. Vern W. Mc Gee (Austin: Univ. of Texas Press, 1986) 109.

donde son los cantantes trades in the myth of the individual for the myth of writing. On its blank edges, there lurks desire, promise and curse of the letter's renewal.

When Foucault died, Sarduy wrote that he wished he could have given him one of the bits of cotton used to clean *Las meninas,* "por puro fetichismo... como el cartílago que se venera del esqueleto disperso de un santo."[20] For Sarduy, Foucault, historian of sexuality, wanted to suspend desire, to override its anguish, to emulate the Buddhist flight from the maelstrom of samsara, the going around in circles which is the lot of the living, perhaps the lot of writing, certainly the lot of any representation. From a privileged, and limited, vantage point in Latin American letters, Sarduy's works rewrite the possibility of such a suspension, neither solemn, nor nihilistic bracketing of desire, representation, irony. In *De donde son los cantantes,* the slow-burn of the fading subject and the blurred inscription of the gestures of writing open the space of that bracketing, intermittent replay between inscription and its absence, littoral region of the letter, *Cobra, Maitreya, La simulación, Colibrí,* a crossing of desire with its desired suspension, a marginal, yet fruitful legacy, a going thing.

---

[20] "Un algodón de 'Las meninas' para Michel Foucault," *El País* [Madrid] 27 June 1984: 35.

SELECTED BIBLIOGRAPHY

1: BY SEVERO SARDUY

"Un algodón de 'Las meninas' para Michel Foucault." *El País* 27 June 27 1984: 35.
Barroco. Buenos Aires: Sudamericana, 1974.
"El barroco y el neobarroco." *América Latina en su literatura.* Ed. César Fernández Moreno. Mexico: Siglo XXI, 1972. 167-184.
Big Bang. Barcelona: Tusquets, 1974.
Cobra. Buenos Aires: Editorial Sudamericana, 1972.
Colibrí. Barcelona: Argos Vergara, 1984.
"Conversación con Severo Sarduy." With Emir Rodríguez Monegal. *Revista de Occidente* 93 (1970): 315-343.
"Conversation with Seudo Severo: A Dialogue." With Dennis Seager. *Dispositio* 5-6.15-16 (1980-81): 129-142.
De donde son los cantantes. Mexico: Mortiz, 1967. Barcelona: Barral, 1980.
"Dos décimas revolucionarias." *Nueva Generación, Revolución* 13 January 1959: 5.
"L'Ecriture autonome." Rev. of French translation of *Cien años de soledad.* By Gabriel García Márquez. *La Quinzaine Littéraire* 63 (1968): 3-4. Review appears in English in *Review 70* (Center for Inter-American Relations): 171-174.
"En su centro." *Nueva Generación, Revolución* 28 January 1959: 15.
"Entre les 'arrivés' et l'avant-garde." *La Quinzaine Littéraire* 126 (1971): 13-14.
"Entrevista con Severo Sarduy." With Jean M. Fossey. *Ínsula* 303 (1972): 4.
"Entrevista con Severo Sarduy." With Efraín Hurtado. *Actual: Revista de la Universidad de los Andes* 2.5 (1969): 123-128.
Escrito sobre un cuerpo. Buenos Aires: Sudamericana, 1969.
"Las estructuras de la narración. Diálogo." With Emir Rodríguez Monegal. *Mundo Nuevo* 2 (1966): 15-26. As "Severo Sarduy." *El arte de narrar.* Ed. Rodríguez Monegal. Caracas: Monte Ávila, 1968. 269-292.
Gestos. Barcelona: Barral, 1963.
"Interview: Severo Sarduy." With Roberto González Echevarría. *Diacritics* 2.2 (1972): 41-45.
Maitreya. Barcelona: Barral, 1978.
"Los métodos de un crítico." *Imagen,* Suplemento No. 30 (1968): 9-16.

"Notas a las notas a las notas . . . a propósito de Manuel Puig." *Revista Iberoamericana* 37.76-77 (1971): 555-567.
Para la voz. Madrid: Espiral, 1977.
"Un Proust cubain." Rev. of French translation of *Paradiso*, by José Lezama Lima. *La Quinzaine Littéraire* 115 (1971): 3-4.
La simulación. Caracas: Monte Ávila, 1982.
"Sur Gongora." *Tel Quel* 25 (1965): 91-93.
"Tanger." *Tel Quel* 47 (1971): 86-88.
"Todo por convencer." *Hispamérica* 3 (1973): 39-43.
"Tu dulce nombre halagará mi oído." *Homenaje a Gertrudis Gómez de Avellaneda. Memorias del Simposio en el Centenario de su muerte*. Ed. Gladys Zaldívar, and Rosa Martínez Cabrera. Miami: Universal, 1981. 19-21.

2: ABOUT SARDUY

Alzola, Concepción. "Verba Cubanorum: El habla popular cubana en *De Dónde Son los Cantantes* [sic]." *Cinco aproximaciones a la narrativa hispano americana contemporánea*. Ed. Gladys Zaldívar. Madrid: Colección Nova Scholar, 1977. 11-81.
Barrenechea, Ana María. "Severo Sarduy o la aventura textual." *Narradores hispanoamericanos de hoy: Simposio*. Univ. of North Carolina Studies in the Romance Languages and Literatures 1. Chapel Hill: Departament of Romance Languages, 1973. Rpt. in Barrenechea, *Textos hispano-americanos: de Sarmiento a Sarduy*. Caracas: Monte Ávila, 1978. 221-234.
Barthes, Roland. "La Face Baroque." *La Quinzaine Littéraire* 28 (1967): 13. In Spanish in *Mundo Nuevo* 14 (1967): 70-71.
Bush, Andrew. "Huellas de la danza: gestos primeros del barroco sarduyano." *Historia y ficción en la narrativa hispanoamericana*. Ed. Roberto González Echevarría. Caracas: Monte Ávila, 1984. 333-342.
Carrera, Arturo. "El juego de las simpatías." *Hispamérica* 2 (1972): 19-26.
Christ, Ronald. "The New Latin American Novel." *Partisan Review* 42 (1975): 459-463.
Conte, Rafael. "Severo Sarduy, entre el juego y la transgresión." *Informaciones* 15 April 1971: 1-2.
Couffon, Claude. "Severo Sarduy et la réalité cubaine." *Les Lettres Françaises* 22 May 1967: 9-10.
Cozarinski, Edgardo. "Un espacio verbal llamado Cuba." *Sur*, 312 (1968): 69-70.
Feito, Francisco E. "Severo Sarduy en la actual narrativa hispanoamericana." *El Urogallo* 2.8 (1971): 94-97.
Fossey, Jean M. "Severo Sarduy: Del 'boom' al 'big-bang.'" *Índice*, 333 (1973): 55-59. Also in *Review 74* 6-12.
Foster, David W. "Severo Sarduy" [bibliography]. *Cuban Literature: A Research Guide* (New York: Garland, 1985). 444-450.
Franco, Jean. "The Crisis of the Liberal Imagination and the Utopia of Writing." *Ideologies and Literature* [Minnesota] 1.1 (1976-77): 5-24.
González Echevarría, Roberto. "In Search of the Lost Center." *Review 72* (Center for Inter-American Relations) 6 (1972): 28-31.
———. *Isla a su vuelo fugitiva. Ensayos críticos sobre literatura hispanoamericana*. Madrid: Porrúa, 1983.
———. "Memoria de apariencias y ensayo de *Cobra*." *Relecturas: estudios de literatura cubana*. Caracas: Monte Ávila, 1976. 129-152.

González Echevarría, Roberto. "Para una bibliografía de y sobre Severo Sarduy, (1955-1971)." *Revista Iberoamericana* 38.79 (1972): 333-343. Updated in *Severo Sarduy*. Ed. Julián Ríos. (Madrid: Espiral, Fundamentos, 1976), and in *La ruta de Severo Sarduy*.
———. "El primer relato de Severo Sarduy." *Revista Iberoamericana* 48.118-119 (1982): 73-90. Also in *Isla a su vuelo fugitiva* 123-144.
———. "Rehearsal for Cobra." *Review 74* (Center for Inter-American Relations) (1974): 38-44.
———. *La ruta de Severo Sarduy* (Hanover, N.H.: Ediciones del Norte, 1987. Includes a selected Sarduy bibliography.
———. "Son de La Habana: la ruta de Severo Sarduy." *Revista Iberoamericana* 37.76-77 (1971): 725-740.
Johndrow, Donald R. " 'Total' Reality in Severo Sarduy's Search for *Lo Cubano*." *Romance Notes* 13 (1972): 445-452.
Levine, Suzanne Jill. "Two Writers of the Neo-Baroque." *Latin American Literary Review* 2 (1974): 25-37.
———. "Discourse as Bricolage." *Review 74* (Center for Inter-American Relations) (1974): 32-37.
MacAdam, Alfred. "Severo Sarduy: Vital Signs." *Modern Latin American Narratives: The Dreams of Reason*. Chicago: Univ. of Chicago Press, 1977. 44-50.
Mace, Marie-Anne. "La Face française de Severo Sarduy." *Recherches et Etude Comparatistes Ibero-Françaises de la Sorbonne* 3 (1981): 87-93.
Martínez, Tomás Eloy. "El lenguage, ese libidinoso." *Primera Plana* 340 (1969): 59.
Méndez Rodenas, Adriana. "Erotismo, cultura y sujeto en *De donde son los cantantes*." *Revista Iberoamericana* 44.102-103 (1978): 45-63.
———. "La imagen histórica en la novela de la Revolución cubana: realismo y barroco." Diss. Cornell Univ., 1979.
———. *Severo Sarduy: El neobarroco de la transgresión*. México: Universidad Nacional Autónoma de México, 1983.
Menton, Seymor. *Prose Fiction of the Cuban Revolution*. Austin: Univ. of Texas Press, 1975.
Miranda, Julio C. "El nuevo pensamiento cubano." *El Urogallo* 2.8 (1971): 84-93.
———. *Nueva literatura cubana*. Madrid: Taurus, 1971.
Ortega, Julio. "Nota sobre Sarduy." *La contemplación y la fiesta*. Caracas: Monte Ávila, 1969. 205-211. Also as "Severo Sarduy." *Relato de la utopía*. By Ortega. Barcelona: La Gaya Ciencia, 1973). 161-172.
Prieto, René. "La ambiviolencia en la obra de Severo Sarduy." *Cuadernos americanos* [año 44] 258.1 (1985): 241-253.
Ríos, Julián, ed. *Severo Sarduy*. Madrid: Espiral/Fundamentos, 1976.
Rivero Potter, Alicia. "Algunas metáforas somáticas – erótico-escripturales en *De donde son los cantantes* y *Cobra*." *Revista Iberoamericana* 49.123-124 (1983): 497-507.
Rodríguez-Luis, Julio. "Sobre los cantantes de Severo Sarduy." *Ínsula* 303 (1972): 4-5.
Rodríguez Monegal, Emir. "Carnaval/ Antropofagia/ Parodia." *Revista Iberoamericana*, 45.108-109 (1979): 401-412.
———. "Las metamorfosis del texto." *Severo Sarduy*. Ed. J. Ríos 35-61. As "Sarduy: las metamorfosis del éxito." *Narradores de esta América*. 2nd ed. 2 vols. Buenos Aires: Alfa, 1974. 2: 421-445. And in English, "Metamorphoses of the text." *Review 74* (Center for Inter-American Relations) (1974): 16-22.

Santí, Enrico Mario. "Textual Politics: Severo Sarduy." *Latin American Literary Review* 8.16 (1980) 152-160.
Schulman, Ivan. "Severo Sarduy." *Narrativa y crítica de nuestra América.* Ed. Joaquín Roy. Madrid: Castalia, 1978. 387-404.
Sollers, Philippe. "La boca obra." *Tel Quel* 42 (1970): 35-36.
Sucre, Guillermo. "Severo Sarduy: los plenos poderes de la retórica." *Imagen* [Caracas] 20 (1968): 24.
Ulloa, Justo C. "Contenido y *forma yoruba* en 'La Dolores Rondón' de Severo Sarduy." *Homenaje a Lydia Cabrera.* Ed. Reinaldo Sánchez et al. Miami: Universal, 1978. 241-250.
——. "La narrativa de Lezama Lima y Sarduy: Entre la imagen visionaria y el juego verbal." Diss. Univ. Kentucky, 1973.
——. "Severo Sarduy: pintura y literatura." *Hispamérica,* 14.41 (1985): 85-94.
——, and Leonor A. de Ulloa. "Leyendo las huellas de Auxilio y Socorro." *Hispamérica* 4.10 (1975): 9-24.
——. "Proyecciones y ramificaciones del deseo en "Junto al río de Cenizas de rosa.' " *Revista Iberoamericana* 41.92-93 (1975): 569-578.

3. WORKS CONSULTED

Alonso, Gladys, and Fernández, Ángel Luis, eds. *Antología de lingüística cubana.* 2 vols. La Habana: Editorial de Ciencias Sociales, 1977.
Arnott, Peter. *The Theatres of Japan.* New York: St. Martin's Press, 1969.
Bakhtin, Mikhail. *La poétique de Dostoievski.* Trans. Isabelle Kolitcheff. Paris: Seuil, 1970. *Problems of Dostoevsky's Poetics.* Trans. R. W. Rotsel. U.S.A.: Ardis, 1973.
——. *Speech Genres and Other Late Essays.* Trans. Vern W. Mc Gee. Austin: Univ. Texas Press, 1985.
Booth, Wayne, C. *The Rhetoric of Fiction.* Chicago: The Univ. of Chicago Press, 1961.
Barthes, Roland. "Bibliographie critique." *Communication* 4 (1964): 136-144.
——. *Camera Lucida: Reflections on Photography.* Trans. Richard Howard. New York: Hill and Wang, 1981.
——. *Critique et Vérité.* Paris: Seuil, 1966.
——. *Le Degré zéro de l'écriture.* 1953. Paris: Seuil, 1972.
——. *Eléments de sémiologie.* Paris: Gonthier, 1964.
——. *L'Empire des signes.* Geneva: Skira, 1970.
——. *Essais Critiques.* Paris: Seuil, 1964.
——. *Fragments d'un discours amoureux.* Paris: Seuil, 1977.
——. "Introduction à l'analyse structurale des récits," *Communications* 8 (1966): 1-27.
——. "Jeunes Chercheurs." *Communications* 19 (1972): 1+.
——. *Mythologies.* Paris: Seuil, 1957.
——. *Le Plaisir du texte.* Paris: Seuil, 1973.
——. *Roland Barthes.* Paris: Seuil, 1975.
——. *S/Z.* Paris: Seuil, 1970.
Benjamin, Walter. *Charles Baudelaire: A Lyric Poet in the Era of High Capitalism.* Trans. Harry Zohn. London: NLB, 1973.
——. *The Origin of German Tragic Drama.* Trans. John Osborne. London: NLB, 1977.
——. *Reflections: Essays, Aphorisms, Autobiographical Writings.* Trans. Edmund Jephcott. New York: Harcourt, 1978.
Benveniste, Emile. *Problèmes de la linguistique générale.* Paris: Gallimard, 1966.

SELECTED BIBLIOGRAPHY

Bloom, Harold. "Freud y lo sublime: una teoría catástrofe de la creatividad." Trans. Philip Metzidakis. *Escandalar* 1.1 (1978): 18-30.
Borges, Jorge Luis. Prólogo. *La invención de Morel.* By Adolfo Bioy Casares. 1968. Madrid: Alianza, 1972, 9-12.
Calvet, Louis-Jean. *Roland Barthes: un regard politique sur le signe.* Paris: Payot, 1973.
Carpentier, Alejo. *La música en Cuba.* México: Fondo de Cultura Económica, 1946.
Clément, Catherine, et al. *Jacques Derrida. L'Arc* 54 (1973). Issue dedicated to the work of Derrida.
DeGeorge, Richard, and Fernande DeGeorge, eds. *The Structuralists: From Marx to Lévi-Strauss.* Garden City, N. Y.: Doubleday, 1972.
Deleuze, Gilles, and Félix Guattari. *Anti-Oedipus: Capitalism and Schizophrenia.* Trans. R. Hurley, M. Seem, and H. R. Lane. Preface by M. Foucault. Minneapolis: Univ. Minnesota Press, 1977.
De Man, Paul. *Allegories of Reading: Figural Language in Rousseau, Nietzsche, Rilke, and Proust.* New Haven: Yale Univ. Press, 1979.
Derrida, Jacques. *La dissémination.* Paris: Seuil, 1972.
———. *L'écriture et la différence.* Paris: Seuil, 1967.
———. *De la grammatologie.* Paris: Minuit, 1967.
———. *Of Grammatology.* Trans. Gayatri C. Spivak. Baltimore: Johns Hopkins Univ. Press, 1976.
———. *Positions: Entretiens avec Henri Ronse, Julia Kristeva, Jean-Louis Houdebine, Guy Scarpetta.* Paris: Minuit, 1972.
———. "Sémiologie et grammatologie." *Essays in Semiotics/Essais de sémiotique.* Ed. J. Kristeva, et al. Paris: Mouton, 1971: 11-27.
Ducrot, Oswald, and Tzvetan Todorov. *Dictionnaire encyclopédique des sciences du langage.* Paris: Seuil, 1972.
Echavarren, Roberto. "On Literariness." *Che Voui? In the Freudian Field: Journal of Psychoanalysis* 1.1 (1984): 81-100.
Falk, Eugene H. *Types of Thematic Structure.* Chicago: The Univ. of Chicago Press, 1967.
Fernández, Macedonio. *Manera de una psique sin cuerpo.* Barcelona: Tusquets, 1973.
Fitzgerald, John J. *Peirce's Theory of Signs as Foundation for Pragmatism.* The Hague: Mouton, 1966.
Forster, E. M. *Aspects of the Novel.* New York: Harcourt, Brace & World, 1927.
Foucault, Michel. *The Order of Things: an Archaeology of the Human Sciences.* New York: Vintage, 1973. Translation of *Les Mots et les choses.* Paris: Gallimard, 1966.
Freud, Sigmund. *La histeria.* Trans. Luis López-Ballesteros. Madrid: Alianza, 1967.
———. *The Interpretation of Dreams.* Trans. James Strachey. London: Allen & Unwin, 1954.
———. *Obras completas.* 24 vols. Trans. José Etcheverry. Buenos Aires: Amorrortu, 1979. Vol. 14.
Frye, Northrop. *Anatomy of Criticism: Four Essays.* Princeton: Princeton Univ. Press, 1957.
Genette, Gérard. *Figures I, II, III.* Paris: Seuil, 1966, 1969, 1972.
———. *Mimologiques.* Paris: Seuil, 1976.
González Echevarría, Roberto. *The Voice of the Masters: Writing and Authority in Modern Latin American Literature.* Latin American Monographs 64. Austin: Univ. of Texas Press, 1985.

Greimas, A. J. "Les actants, les acteurs, et les figures." *Sémiotique narrative et textuelle.* Ed. Claude Chabrol. Paris: Larousse, 1973. 161-176.
———. *Du sens: essais sémiotique.* Paris: Seuil, 1970.
———. *Semántica estructural: investigación metodológica.* Trans. Alfredo de la Fuente. Madrid: Gredos, 1973. Translation of *Sémantique structurale: Recherches de méthode.* Paris: Larousse, 1966.
Guillén, Nicolás. *Obra poética, 1920-1958.* La Habana: Instituto Cubano del Libro, 1972.
Heath, Stephen. *Vertige du déplacement: lecture de Barthes.* Paris: Fayard, 1974.
Heidegger, Martin. *On the Way to Language.* Trans. Peter D. Hertz. New York: Harper & Row, 1971.
Jakobson, Roman. *Essais de linguistique générale.* Trans. Nicolas Ruwet. Paris: Minuit, 1963.
———. *Fundamentals of Language.* The Hague: Mouton, 1956.
———. *Shifters, Verbal Categories, and the Russian Verb.* Cambridge: Harvard Univ. Press, 1957.
Jameson, Fredric. *The Prison-House of Language.* Princeton: Princeton University Press, 1972.
Kawatake, Toshio. *A History of Japanese Theater.* Japan: Kokusai Bunka Shinkokai [Japan Cultural Society], 1971.
Klein, Richard. "Prolegomenon to Derrida." *Diacritics* 2 (1972): 29-34.
Kristeva, Julia, et al. *Essays in Semiotics/Essais de sémiotique.* Paris: Mouton, 1971.
———. "Une poétique ruinée." *La poétique de Dostoievski.* By Mikhail Bakhtine. Trans. I. Kolitcheff. Paris: Seuil, 1970. 5-27.
———. *Le Révolution du langage poétique.* Paris: Seuil, 1974.
———. *Sémiotikè: Recherches pour une sémanalyse.* Paris: Seuil, 1969.
———. *Le texte du roman: approche sémiologique d'une structure discursive transformationnelle.* Paris: Mouton, 1970.
Lacan, Jacques. *Ecrits I.* 1966. Paris: Seuil, 1970.
———. *Ecrits II.* 1966. Paris: Seuil, 1971.
———. *The Language of the Self: The Function of Language in Psychoanalysis.* Trans. Anthony Wilden. Baltimore: The Johns Hopkins Univ. Press, 1968.
———. *Les quatre concepts fondamentaux de la psychanalyse.* Livre XI. 1964. Paris: Seuil, 1973.
Lemon, Lee T., and Marion J. Reis, trans. *Russian Formalist Critics.* Lincoln: Univ. of Nebraska Press, 1965.
Laporte, Roger. "L'empire des signifiants." *Critique* 28 (1972): 538-594.
Lawrence, D. H. *Psychoanalysis of the Unconscious. Fantasia of the Unconscious.* Intro. Philip Rieff. 1921, 1922. New York: Viking, 1960.
Lévi-Strauss, Claude. *The Savage Mind.* Trans. George Weidenfeld. London: Weidenfeld & Nicolson, 1966.
———. *Tristes tropiques.* Paris: Plon, 1955.
Lotringer, Sylvère. "Argo-Notes: Roland Barthes' Textual Trip." *Boundary* 2 (1974): 562-572.
———. "The Game of the Name." *Diacritics* 3 (1973): 2-9.
Lubbock, Percy. *The Craft of Fiction.* 1921. New York: Viking, 1957.
Mañac, Jorge. *Indagación al choteo.* 1940. Miami Mnemosyne, 1969.
Morot-Sir, Edouard. *La pensée française d'aujour'hui.* Paris: Presses Univ. de France, 1971.
Muñoz Millanes, José. "El 'concepto' de la alegoría." *Linguistica e Letteratura* 6.2 (1981): 87-119.

Nasio, J. D., and Taillandier, G. "Fragments sur le semblant." *Ornicar?* 5 (1975/76): 88-92.
Nietzsche, Friedrich. *The Birth of Tragedy* and *The Case of Wagner.* Trans. Walter Kaufmann. New York. Vintage, 1967.
——. *The Portable Nietzsche.* Trans., ed. Walter Kaufmann. New York: Viking, 1954.
Ogden, C. K., and I. A. Richards. *The Meaning of Meaning.* 8th ed., rev. New York: Harcourt, Brace, 1947.
Ortiz, Fernando. *Hampa Afro-Cubana: Los Negros brujos.* 1906. Miami: Ed. Universal, 1973.
——. *Nuevo catauro de cubanismos.* 1923. La Habana: Editorial de Ciencias Sociales, 1975.
Peirce, Charles, S. *Collected Papers* Ed. Charles Hartshorne, and Paul Weiss. Cambridge: Harvard Univ. Press, 1934. Vol. 5.
Pérez Firmat, *Literature and Liminality: Festive Readings in the Hispanic Tradition.* Durham: Duke University Press, 1986.
Rama, Ángel. *Más allá del boom. Literatura y mercado.* Mexico: Marcha Editores, 1981.
Récanati, François. "Histoire rétrospective de la théorie du signe." Typescript of lectures given at the Ecole des Hautes Etudes, Paris. 14 Nov. 1975 to 21 May 1976.
Ricardou, Jean. *Problèmes du Nouveau Roman.* Paris: Seuil, 1967.
Rifflet-Lemaire, Anika. *Jacques Lacan.* Bruxelles: Dessart, 1970.
Roudinesco, Elisabeth. "A propos du 'concept' de l'écriture: Lecture de Jacques Derrida." *La Nouvelle Critique* 39 bis (1970): 219-230.
Salgado, María. A. "El arte de las leyendas en Gertrudis Gómez de Avellaneda." *Homenaje a Gertrudis Gómez de Avellaneda, loc. cit.* 338-346.
Sartre, Jean-Paul. *Qu'est-ce que la littérature?* Paris: Gallimard, 1948.
Saussure, Ferdinand de. *Cours de linguistique générale.* Ed. Taulio de Mauro. 1915. Paris: Payot, 1972.
Schwartz, Lía Lerner. "En torno a la enunciación en la sátira: los casos de *El Crotalón* y los *Sueños* de Quevedo." *Lexis* 9.2 (1985): 209-227.
Sollers, Philippe. *L'écriture et l'experience des limites.* Paris: Seuil, 1968.
Todorov, Tzvetan, ed. "L'énonciation." *Langages* 17 (1970).
——. *Littérature et signification.* Paris: Larousse, 1967.
——. *Théorie de la littérature.* Paris: Seuil, 1966.
Unamuno, Miguel de. *Cómo se hace una novela.* 1926. Madrid: Alianza, 1978.
Vitier, Cintio. *Lo cubano en la poesía.* 1958. La Habana: Instituto del Libro, 1970.
Wahl, François. "Chute." *Tel Quel* 63 (1975): 34-43.
——. *Qu'est-ce que le structuralisme?* Paris: Seuil, 1973.
Walcutt, Charles Child. *Man's Changing Mask: Modes and Methods of Characterization in Fiction.* Minneapolis: Univ. Minnesota Press, 1966.
Watts, Alan W. *The Spirit of Zen: A way of life, work and art in the Far East.* New York: Grove: 1958.
Wilden, Anthony. "Lacan and the Discourse of the Other." *The Language of the Self: The Function of Language in Psychoanalysis.* By J. Lacan. Trans. A. Wilden. Johns Hopkins Press, 1968. 159-311.

NORTH CAROLINA STUDIES IN THE ROMANCE LANGUAGES AND LITERATURES

I.S.B.N. Prefix 0-8078-

Recent Titles

THE LIFE AND WORKS OF LUIS CARLOS LÓPEZ, by Martha S. Bazik. 1977. (No. 183). *-9183-5.*

"THE CORT D'AMOR". A THIRTEENTH-CENTURY ALLEGORICAL ART OF LOVE, by Lowanne E. Jones. 1977. (No. 185). *-9185-1.*

PHYTONYMIC DERIVATIONAL SYSTEMS IN THE ROMANCE LANGUAGES: STUDIES IN THEIR ORIGIN AND DEVELOPMENT, by Walter E. Geiger. 1978. (No. 187). *-9187-8.*

LANGUAGE IN GIOVANNI VERGA'S EARLY NOVELS, by Nicholas Patruno. 1977. (No. 188). *-9188-6.*

BLAS DE OTERO EN SU POESÍA, by Moraima de Semprún Donahue. 1977. (No. 189). *-9189-4.*

LA ANATOMÍA DE "EL DIABLO COJUELO": DESLINDES DEL GÉNERO ANATOMÍSTICO, por C. George Peale. 1977. (No. 191). *-9191-6.*

RICHARD SANS PEUR, EDITED FROM "LE ROMANT DE RICHART" AND FROM GILLES CORROZET'S "RICHART SANS PAOUR", by Denis Joseph Conlon. 1977. (No. 192). *-9192-4.*

MARCEL PROUST'S GRASSET PROOFS. *Commentary and Variants,* by Douglas Alden. 1978. (No. 193). *-9193-2.*

MONTAIGNE AND FEMINISM, by Cecile Insdorf. 1977. (No. 194). *-9194-0.*

SANTIAGO F. PUGLIA, AN EARLY PHILADELPHIA PROPAGANDIST FOR SPANISH AMERICAN INDEPENDENCE, by Merle S. Simmons. 1977. (No. 195). *-9195-9.*

BAROQUE FICTION-MAKING. A STUDY OF GOMBERVILLE'S "POLEXANDRE", by Edward Baron Turk. 1978. (No. 196). *-9196-7.*

THE TRAGIC FALL: DON ÁLVARO DE LUNA AND OTHER FAVORITES IN SPANISH GOLDEN AGE DRAMA, by Raymond R. MacCurdy. 1978. (No. 197). *-9197-5.*

A BAHIAN HERITAGE. An Ethnolinguistic Study of African Influences on Bahian Portuguese, by William W. Megenney. 1978. (No. 198). *-9198-3.*

"LA QUERELLE DE LA ROSE": Letters and Documents, by Joseph L. Baird and John R. Kane. 1978. (No. 199). *-9199-1.*

TWO AGAINST TIME. *A Study of the Very Present Worlds of Paul Claudel and Charles Péguy,* by Joy Nachod Humes. 1978. (No. 200). *-9200-9.*

TECHNIQUES OF IRONY IN ANATOLE FRANCE. Essay on *Les Sept Femmes de la Barbe-Bleue,* by Diane Wolfe Levy. 1978. (No. 201). *-9201-7.*

THE PERIPHRASTIC FUTURES FORMED BY THE ROMANCE REFLEXES OF "VADO (AD)" PLUS INFINITIVE, by James Joseph Champion. 1978. (No. 202). *-9202-5.*

THE EVOLUTION OF THE LATIN /b/-/ṷ/ MERGER: A Quantitative and Comparative Analysis of the *B-V* Alternation in Latin Inscriptions, by Joseph Louis Barbarino. 1978. (No. 203). *-9203-3.*

METAPHORIC NARRATION: THE STRUCTURE AND FUNCTION OF METAPHORS IN "A LA RECHERCHE DU TEMPS PERDU", by Inge Karalus Crosman. 1978. (No. 204). *-9204-1.*

LE VAIN SIECLE GUERPIR. A Literary Approach to Sainthood through Old French Hagiography of the Twelfth Century, by Phyllis Johnson and Brigitte Cazelles. 1979. (No. 205). *-9205-X.*

THE POETRY OF CHANGE: A STUDY OF THE SURREALIST WORKS OF BENJAMIN PÉRET, by Julia Field Costich. 1979. (No. 206). *-9206-8.*

When ordering please cite the *ISBN Prefix* plus the last four digits for each title.

Send orders to: University of North Carolina Press
P.O. Box 2288
CB# 6215
Chapel Hill, NC 27515-2288
U.S.A.

NORTH CAROLINA STUDIES IN THE ROMANCE LANGUAGES AND LITERATURES

I.S.B.N. Prefix 0-88438

Recent Titles

NARRATIVE PERSPECTIVE IN THE POST-CIVIL WAR NOVELS OF FRANCISCO AYALA "MUERTES DE PERRO" AND "EL FONDO DEL VASO", by Maryellen Bieder. 1979. (No. 207). *-9207-6.*
RABELAIS: HOMO LOGOS, by Alice Fiola Berry. 1979. (No. 208). *-9208-4.*
"DUEÑAS" AND "DONCELLAS": A STUDY OF THE "DOÑA RODRÍGUEZ" EPISODE IN "DON QUIJOTE", by Conchita Herdman Marianella. 1979. (No. 209). *-9209-2.*
PIERRE BOAISTUAU'S "HISTOIRES TRAGIQUES": A STUDY OF NARRATIVE FORM AND TRAGIC VISION, by Richard A. Carr. 1979. (No. 210). *-9210-6.*
REALITY AND EXPRESSION IN THE POETRY OF CARLOS PELLICER, by George Melnykovich. 1979. (No. 211). *-9211-4.*
MEDIEVAL MAN, HIS UNDERSTANDING OF HIMSELF, HIS SOCIETY, AND THE WORLD, by Urban T. Holmes, Jr. 1980. (No. 212). *-9212-2.*
MÉMOIRES SUR LA LIBRAIRIE ET SUR LA LIBERTÉ DE LA PRESSE, introduction and notes by Graham E. Rodmell. 1979. (No. 213). *-9213-0.*
THE FICTIONS OF THE SELF. THE EARLY WORKS OF MAURICE BARRES, by Gordon Shenton. 1979. (No. 214). *-9214-9.*
CECCO ANGIOLIERI. A STUDY, by Gifford P. Orwen. 1979. (No. 215). *-9215-7.*
THE INSTRUCTIONS OF SAINT LOUIS: A CRITICAL TEXT, by David O'Connell. 1979. (No. 216). *-9216-5.*
ARTFUL ELOQUENCE, JEAN LEMAIRE DE BELGES AND THE RHETORICAL TRADITION, by Michael F. O. Jenkins. 1980. (No. 217). *-9217-3.*
A CONCORDANCE TO MARIVAUX'S COMEDIES IN PROSE, edited by Donald C. Spinelli. 1979. (No. 218). 4 volumes, *-9218-1* (set); *-9219-X* (v. 1); *-9220-3* (v. 2); *-9221-1* (v. 3); *-9222-X* (v. 4).
ABYSMAL GAMES IN THE NOVELS OF SAMUEL BECKETT, by Angela B. Moorjani. 1982. (No. 219). *-9223-8.*
GERMAIN NOUVEAU DIT HUMILIS: ÉTUDE BIOGRAPHIQUE, par Alexandre L. Amprimoz. 1983. (No. 220). *-9224-6.*
THE "VIE DE SAINT ALEXIS" IN THE TWELFTH AND THIRTEENTH CENTURIES: AN EDITION AND COMMENTARY, by Alison Goddard Elliot. 1983. (No. 221). *-9225-4.*
THE BROKEN ANGEL: MYTH AND METHOD IN VALÉRY, by Ursula Franklin. 1984. (No. 222). *-9226-2.*
READING VOLTAIRE'S "CONTES": A SEMIOTICS OF PHILOSOPHICAL NARRATION, by Carol Sherman. 1985. (No. 223). *-9227-0.*
THE STATUS OF THE READING SUBJECT IN THE "LIBRO DE BUEN AMOR", by Marina Scordilis Brownlee. 1985. (No. 224). *-9228-9.*
MARTORELL'S "TIRANT LO BLANCH": A PROGRAM FOR MILITARY AND SOCIAL REFORM IN FIFTEENTH-CENTURY CHRISTENDOM, by Edward T. Aylward. 1985. (No. 225). *-9229-7.*
NOVEL LIVES: THE FICTIONAL AUTOBIOGRAPHIES OF GUILLERMO CABRERA INFANTE AND MARIO VARGAS LLOSA, by Rosemary Geisdorfer Feal. 1986. (No. 226). *-9230-0.*
SOCIAL REALISM IN THE ARGENTINE NARRATIVE, by David William Foster. 1986. (No. 227). *-9231-9.*
HALF-TOLD TALES: DILEMMAS OF MEANING IN THREE FRENCH NOVELS, by Philip Stewart. 1987. (No. 228). *-9232-7.*
POLITIQUES DE L'ECRITURE BATAILLE/DERRIDA: le sens du sacré dans la pensée française du surréalisme à nos jours, par Jean-Michel Heimonet. 1987. (No. 229). *-9233-5.*

When ordering please cite the *ISBN Prefix* plus the last four digits for each title.

Send orders to: University of North Carolina Press
P.O. Box 2288
CB# 6215
Chapel Hill, NC 27515-2288
U.S.A.

The Department of Romance Studies Digital Arts and Collaboration Lab at the University of North Carolina at Chapel Hill is proud to support the digitization of the North Carolina Studies in the Romance Languages and Literatures series.